PURPOSEFUL EDUCATION

PURPOSEFUL EDUCATION

My Bet Against *Poverty*

Ebrima B. Sawaneh

Copyright © 2023 by Ebrima B Sawaneh

PURPOSEFUL EDUCATION: My Bet Against Poverty

All rights reserved.

No portion of this book may be reproduced, distributed, or transmitted in any form or by any means, including photocopying, recording, or other electronic or mechanical methods, without the prior written permission of the publisher, except in the case of brief quotations embodied in critical reviews and certain other noncommercial uses permitted by copyright law.

Although these stories are true, in some instances, names may have been changed to protect the privacy of the individuals.

ISBN: 979-8-89109-363-8 - paperback

ISBN: 979-8-89109-364-5 - ebook

DEDICATION

I dedicate this book to my titan of mentors, friends, sponsors, classmates, colleagues, and teachers.

To Ndey Amie Sawo and my K-family – Kumba, Kebba & Khadri Sawaneh, thank you for all the love.

To all those who are struggling or have struggled to acquire knowledge. Either as a learner or a supporter.

Thank you to my parents, Adama Fatty and Alhagie Bunja Sawaneh.

TABLE OF CONTENTS

DEDICATION v

INTRODUCTION ix

PART ONE

Chapter One: Kawsu Goes To School 1

Chapter Two: I Wanted To Drop Out Of School 9

Chapter Three: The Firm And Caring Educator 15

Chapter Four: First Dropped Out Of School 21

Chapter Five: I Became A Carpenter 27

Chapter Six: April 10 & 11 – Where Were You? 39

Chapter Seven: Grade Nine Results 45

PART TWO

Chapter Eight: It Take A Village To Educate A Child . . . 53

Chapter Nine: I Will Not Take Last In This Class 59

Chapter Ten: Collaboration Is Better Than Competition . 71

Chapter Eleven: Final Year In High School 77

Chapter Twelve: It Was Time To Harvest 83

Chapter Thirteen: Life After High School Is Hard 89

Chapter Fourteen: The First Banker From My Village . . .95

PART THREE

Chapter Fifteen: Balancing Work And Study 111

Chapter Sixteen: The Road To Start Marriage. 121

Chapter Seventeen: New Job & New Level 127

Chapter Eighteen: International Job Opportunity 135

Chapter Nineteen: The Road To Nigeria 143

Chapter Twenty: Personal Development Is Personal 151

Chapter Twenty-One: Rise To Arise 157

Afterword: My Experience, Your Learning 165

ACKNOWLEDGEMENTS .169

READ MORE 171

FEEDBACK 173

ABOUT THE AUTHOR 175

INTRODUCTION

According to the Islamic Hadiths, seeking knowledge is an obligation upon every Muslim. However, the pursuit of knowledge should start with the right intention. An intention that should be pure and of benefit to humanity.

I have been lonely at home. Sometimes, I lived on one meal a day. I have celebrated many Eids without new clothing. These experiences made me uncomfortable. Therefore, I acted to change the status quo. Hence, I enrolled in a school. But the invisible hand of poverty continues to thwart my plans.

Three decades of learning have taken so much from me but has given me back even more. I want to share with you the barriers and joys of my learning journey without money. Come with me into the classrooms, village, and offices. The time I was laid and flocked in front of the classroom. The time I dropped out of school. And the time I topped my class at Nusrat High School.

How did I become a chartered accountant after I dropped out of university? We will explore what I believe is the best way to fight poverty. We will meet people on the way: friends, colleagues, relatives, mentors – people who are kind, change agents who bet on me. Because we are all change agents at some point in our lives. We are all purposefully betting against something.

PART ONE

Life does not give us what we deserve.
Life only gives us what we decided.

CHAPTER ONE

KAWSU GOES TO SCHOOL

SARUJA. A small village nestled in the heart of rural Gambia, tended by strong and hardworking farmers, the majority of whom are women. The road that passes through the village was lined with small thatched-roof houses; their walls made of mud blocks. The houses are simple but home to families who have lived in this village for decades.

A majestic cola cordifolia tree stands at the center of the village. The tree is enormous, with branches stretching so wide that they embrace the surrounding area. Under this tree, the village elders have sat together for many years, sharing stories and wisdom. In the night, a masquerade with traditional drums is played. It often hosts the famous Jaliba Kuyateh and his Kumareh bands. The tree there symbolizes the strength and resilience of the natives of Saruja.

Saruja has always been home to many talented individuals who have significantly contributed to national development, including a successful active drama group and a champion regional football team. Saruja has produced experts in many areas, like agriculture, commerce, and governance, to name a few.

This village may be small, but it is a vibrant and thriving community, rich in culture and tradition. It is a place where people live in harmony with nature and each other, a reminder of a simpler way of life. Saruja is where my life began.

SEPTEMBER 1991. Another season of children returning to school from summer break. One morning, I woke up to the peaceful silence of a quiet environment. Opening my eyes, I noticed the soft, natural light filtering through the windows, casting a warm glow on the room. The air was fresh and crisp, filled with the gentle sounds of nature. I took a deep breath, savoring the peace and tranquility of the moment. There were no distractions, just the calm serenity of the present. I felt ready to tackle the day ahead.

But when I stepped out the door to look at what the other boys were doing that morning, I did not find any of my agemates. The compound was silent. The only sounds were the birds chirping on the big mango tree and the rustling of leaves in the gentle breeze. All the boys in our compound were enrolled in the Brikamaba Primary School in the village next to ours.

At that time, I was living with Jonkon, my maternal grandmother's younger sister. I had lived with Jonkon for a while. In our culture, when toddlers are old enough to stop breastfeeding, it's customary to send them to stay with their grandparents

INTRODUCTION

for a while before they return home to their parents. It was at that age that I had moved in with my grandmother's sister.

Although I reached an age where I could start going to school, Grandmother Jonkon wanted me to start classes after I returned to my parents' house. For two weeks, there was a deep ache in my chest, a gnawing emptiness that couldn't be filled. Even when surrounded by people, I couldn't shake the feeling that I was entirely alone.

I wanted to go to school and make friends like the other children. But my grandma would not let me enroll in school. I felt sad every morning when I saw the other children as they left for school dressed in their smart, crisp white short-sleeved shirts paired with sleek black shorts. To make matters worse, these children always talked about their school food: jollof rice with canned beef on top. On Fridays, the pupils are given big red fried pancakes to bring home. We eat these foods only once a month if we are lucky.

My interest grew more acute with every deadening day until one day I had an inspirational thought: I should follow the boys to school.

One Monday morning, as the week was starting, the cold weather made my grandmother oversleep and lose track of the time she was supposed to wake up. Like a thief in the night, I quickly fetched cool water from a jar and hurriedly bathed while she snored. I dressed in my best clothes, and without a book or school bag, left the compound through the back gate so that no one would suspect my plan. After walking about a kilometer from the village, I saw some of the pupils from our community trekking to school. I heard someone screaming my name as I approached these young boys and a few girls. "Hey, hey, hey! Kawsu is following us!" "It seems he wants to go to school," Bala said.

Everyone immediately stopped. The eldest of the troop, Saikou, asked if my grandmother knew I was going to school, to which I responded, "No," in a sad voice. I worried he would ask me to go back home. He thought momentarily and decided that I could follow them to the school. He must have been concerned about my grandmother and great-grandmother, who would not eat their food without my presence. These ladies loved me and would not even allow me to follow the other boys to the bush to fetch firewood, like in the story of Prophet Yusuf and his brothers.

While we walked together, we chatted about classes, and I felt excited to be conversing with my mates. We talked about football tournaments as well. I tried as much as possible not to sound odd among the others. We walked into the school in a group, and I felt excited to be stepping into a school for the first time. However, a sense of fear also resided within me. I was afraid the schoolteacher would reprimand me and send me out of the class for coming to school without proper registration and a uniform. I was afraid that my grandmother would follow me to school and angrily take me out of class.

Midway across the school grounds, other students approached their respective classrooms. I didn't know where I belonged, so I followed Bala, the youngest boy, to his classroom. We were almost the same age, but he won't ever agree;

he was just a year older than me. When the lessons were about to start, the teacher suddenly noticed my lack of uniform.

"Hello dear, what is your name?"

"My name is Kawsu." I stood up immediately. I felt nervous and elated at the same time.

"Kawsu. Would you like to join this class?" She tilted her head to my height and smiled a wide smile.

"Yes, ma'am," I replied politely.

I had an excellent experience on my first day of school. When we took a break during the day, several children paired up in groups and ate their lunch while others talked about the village football tournament. I just sat and watched them with a smile, believing I would make friends one day.

I trekked back home after school with the pupils I had followed there that morning. We chatted on our way back, sharing our experiences and discussing events that might have happened in some classes.

I arrived home and found my grandmother sitting on the veranda, looking around furiously. When I approached our room, happily chatting with the other kids, my eyes set on her, and I quickly moved behind the tallest boy to hide from her. Judging from the look on her face, I could even tell, before entering the house, how disappointed she felt that I had snuck out to school without her permission, as she did not want me to go to school at that time. We both knew she was not well, and raising the money to send me to school would be hard for her.

"You, Kawsu Sawaneh, why are you hiding? I am going to send you back to your parents' house!" She said angrily, "I can't afford education for you. I don't have enough money to pay for your uniform, books, or daily school lunch allowance."

I could tell how unhappy she was.

My great-grandmother offered me food to eat, but I refused. I felt sad that it was my first and last day in school. For the rest of the day, I tried my best to make her get over being angry with me, but I could not change her mind. I decided I would stay with her and stay away from school. I didn't want to be stubborn about it. Though I made my decision, I knew I would miss the experience of learning and making friends, and would return to being lonely again.

The next morning, she woke up earlier than me, lit some wood, and warmed some water for me to take a bath.

"Kawsu! Kawsu!" exclaimed Grandma in a low tone as she stood beside my bed, gently shaking my shoulder. "It's time for school, and everyone is preparing. Are you not going to school today?"

I quickly sat upright and my eyes opened like someone bitten by an ant. I looked at both sides of the bed to be sure it was not a dream.

"Yes, I will go. I will go. "

Overjoyed, I ran off to prepare for school, excited that my dreams had risen again.

I knew it was a difficult decision for my grandmother to make. Still, she did it to make me happy, and I was grateful for her laying the foundation of my education.

I started going to school, and just as I had hoped, I made friends too. During our breaks, I joined the other boys on the field to run around, sometimes playing football. The early primary classes were a breeze. We spent more time on fun activities like singing and playing football than on academic subjects.

YEAR 2. During one memorable session, my name was changed. The name my parents gave me is Kawsu, after my father's uncle, and that day, the teacher taught us about Islamic traditions and naming practices in the Gambia. She explained that it is common in the villages to have two names: one given during the official naming ceremony, and the other granted by friends of the mother.

"What's your name?" she asked, moving towards my desk.

"Kawsu," I replied.

"That is a nice name. Do you have a second name?" She asked.

I responded with my second name, Ebrima, which my grandmother once told me.

"Do you know the name Ebrima has a great place in Islam? It is the name of the father of the prophets. It's a great name; you should be using that." I nodded affirmatively. I liked my new name and preferred it better than Kawsu.

She changed my name on the school records from Kawsu to Ebrima. My parents had no idea my name was changed at the school. Neither were literate in English. Therefore, there was little chance for them to know about my new name.

It wasn't until I was in seventh grade that my father discovered my new name. My father didn't take it that well at first, but as time went on, he got used to it and adapted because it was written on my papers. However, even today, he only calls me Pa Kawsu, meaning Daddy Kawsu, because I am named after his paternal uncle, who is also called Dad in the Gambian tradition.

CHAPTER TWO

I WANTED TO DROP OUT OF SCHOOL

After the second year in school, my grandmother returned me to my parents and took my younger sister, Jonkon Jr, may her soul rest in peace, who was named after her. Grandma was relocating from the village to the city of Bakoteh, and she needed a girl who could help with household chores and other activities. Additionally, I was already growing up, and my parents needed me to return home to support my father on his farms and to train me. In the village, boys cultivate the farms with their fathers and fetch firewood for their mothers. This use of sons as support workers has led some parents not to send their sons to school.

After I moved back to my parent's house, my father didn't show much support for me to continue going to school. Although he did not stop me from attending school, my educational needs were not his priority either. I felt his inability to finance the daily allowances, uniforms, and other school needs partly contributed to his lack of strong support. Still, I believed there was a part of him that did not like Western education.

Like most other village farmers, whenever the farm work became intense, my father occasionally asked us to work on the farm and miss school for a day or two. For him, missing class for a day was not critical. It was a tough decision, as the family also needed to produce something to let us eat when we returned from school. On the other hand, he has shown keen interest in the Quranic night classes we had attended in the neighboring compound.

On the other hand, my mom was always there, despite her limited earnings. She woke up each morning to prepare breakfast—made of our traditional grinded rice with peanuts, sometimes with sugar, and milk added to give it a long-lasting taste. We called it "Tiya Churo." She sometimes gave me an allowance from her savings as high as 50 bututs. I am unsure whether she believed in the Western education system. But it was clear that she wanted her first son to be happy, like other children in the village. At that period, attending school was the only means to my happiness.

Mariama, my maternal grandmother, is a wealth of stories and wisdom. She had a way of making even the most mundane tasks sound like grand adventures. One of her favorite stories was about my mother's hard work and determination on the farms. She describes how my mother would wake up before the sun rose and work tirelessly on the farm. She would toil under the scorching sun to ensure I would have the best clothes for my initiatory rites.

Grandma Mariama's words painted a vivid picture for me of my mother's dedication. I could almost see her out there in the fields, sweat glistening on her forehead, a determined look on her face. Her stories instilled in me a deep respect and appreciation for the sacrifices my mother made for me.

Malick, my elder half-brother, and Sainabou, my cousin's sister, were going to school and progressing very well. Their presence and performance in the school also gave me some motivation and foresight.

The early years in primary school were exciting. I made new friends from the surrounding villages, and I enjoyed the school extracurricular activities.

However, the challenging time in my primary school life began when a substitute teacher took charge of my class in the fourth grade. Our class teacher, Miss Khan, was to be absent from school, so Mr Bee, a substitute teacher, was asked to step in. Mr Bee asked us to recite and memorize the multiplication table, and anyone who failed to do it correctly would be duly punished.

Like a judgment day, Mr Bee strode confidently into the classroom, a stick freshly plucked from the earth in hand. As he approached the desk, students stood in unison, greeting him with respect and trepidation. With a sharp rap of the stick against the desk, the class fell silent, ready for the lesson to begin.

He reminded us of the punishment if we didn't recite the table correctly. Mr Bee explained to us that whoever failed to recite correctly would be stretched on the table, and the other students would hold onto their legs and hands while they were being flogged.

I was among the first children who were asked to recite the multiplication table from two to six. It was scary, as none of us wanted to be beaten in front of our classmates.

There was so much tension in the room as we recited the multiplication table while the teacher stood with a freshly cut cane. The fear of the consequences of missing recitation will even make you forget what you remembered. I tried to ensure I wouldn't be the victim, but I couldn't hold on for long when I made the first mistake. He immediately stopped me.

I was laid prone on the cold, hard table, my body tense, and trembling as the cruel instrument of punishment descended upon me again and again. The biting sting of the cane on my flesh was a constant, merciless assault as my classmates stood by, some counting each strike with dispassionate detachment while others held me down, pinning me to the table for the comfort of the educator. I was trapped in a whirlwind of pain and humiliation while my cries echoed through the silent classroom.

The bitter taste of humiliation lingered in my mouth as I sat in class, my classmates snickering and whispering behind my back. I couldn't believe the defeat and embarrassment washing over me in that moment. I had always loved learning, but at that moment, I hated school passionately. My parents had never given me such a harsh punishment before, and I couldn't help but regret ever returning to school. Mr Bee, who had inflicted this embarrassment upon me, embodied my hatred towards school. All my passion and enthusiasm for learning died at that moment.

At that time, hitting students with a cane or hand was normal in the Gambian school system. Many young people in the village had been beaten, some even injured, yet nothing was done about it. Most parents believed that if a teacher beat a child at school, it was in the child's best interest. Complaints from parents about teachers beating their children were rare, and some parents even reported their children's misbehavior at home to the teachers. The teachers were like police or Gods, and the students were more afraid of them than the meanest parent at home.

I felt sad and embarrassed for days but could not tell any of this to my parents because I feared that they would not do anything about it. For some time, I thought of dropping out of school but changed my mind. I could not afford to drop out, as we had only one primary school in more than seven villages. I consoled myself but continued to fear Mr Bee throughout my remaining years in primary school.

As I reflect on that experience, I believe the teacher had no issue with me. He wanted us to take education seriously and had to set an example using the existing punishment mechanism. I was one of the examples. I am grateful that such harmful methods of discipline have been banned in our country. Knowing that future generations will not have to endure the same treatment brings me peace.

CHAPTER THREE

THE FIRM AND CARING EDUCATOR

As I progressed through the senior primary classes, the curriculum grew increasingly complex and challenging. Along with these new academic demands, I took on additional responsibilities, such as managing a designated section of the school garden plot. This was a lot to handle, especially when combined with my other interests and home tasks, like playing football, hunting, and farming. Despite the added pressures, I tried my best to stay focused and motivated, as I was determined to succeed academically and in my other pursuits.

I struggled against poverty throughout my fifth and sixth year of primary school. Our farming activities provided enough food to sustain us through the lean times, making it almost impossible to afford most school requirements. The daily school allowance was a luxury that I could not afford.

In addition to farming, my father was a night security officer at Sapu, an agricultural campus just a few kilometers from our village. As a young boy, I often trekked to the campus after school to bring him his dinner. The campus was home to many educated extension workers, most of whom held diplomas and even bachelor's degrees in agriculture. They were privileged compared to most families in our village. They had official government cars and drivers to take their children to and from school, while we walked about seven kilometers daily.

Although the campus residents were kind to us, their children sometimes looked down on us as "poor children." They had access to luxuries such as electricity, tap water, and official cars, while we made do with candles, firewood, donkey carts, and a few bicycles. Despite the stark differences in our lifestyles, the lives of the Sapu campus employees were one of the inspirations for my interest in education. I firmly believed that if I worked hard and got good grades, the campus would provide me with a job as soon as I graduated from high school.

Nonetheless, the pursuit of education continued to be filled with excitement and uncertainty, even in the final year of primary school. During our primary school years, we had World Food Program (WFP) support through the Government of Gambia, where WFP provided more than enough food to schools. The male students were tasked with fetching firewood from the bush, while the girls were responsible for cleaning the classrooms and fetching drinking water in large plastic buckets.

However, to eat the food the government provides, all the children must contribute money, just under 50 bututs per day. This was a token for the students from wealthy homes, but a significant expense for many other children in my village and me. And I couldn't afford that amount of money every day. It was demotivating for me. Yes, I love food, and it was good food. But it was awkward as some children went out for lunch while a few of us remained sitting in class, which confirmed that we could not afford to pay that little contribution. It was painful to know that the firewood I struggled to fetch in the dense forest would be used to cook food I would not get to eat. Although, in some instances, the school offered the teachers' remaining food to pupils who could not eat lunch.

At lunchtime, the class form teacher would call out the names of the pupils who had paid, and they queued up in the cafeteria for their food. Sometimes I was the only person left in class. One day, the class form teacher approached me as I sat alone.

"Hey, Ebrima, why haven't you paid for the school lunch?" Mr Bah asked, "Are your parents giving you money, and you decided to keep it?" He added suspicion.

"No, Mr. Bah." I answered, "I don't have the money and haven't been given the feeding allowance at home."

Mr. Bah asked me to join the rest of the students and eat. I quickly followed the other children before he changed his mind. From that day on, I believe he was observing me closely. Some days I could pay for my lunch and queue up with the other children. But on other days, when I didn't have the money, Mr. Bah would call me and pay my lunch. I remember telling my parents about our schoolteacher, who often pays for my lunch when I didn't have money.

Most students knew Mr. Ebrima Bah as a strict and formidable teacher, but he was much more to me. He was kind and compassionate, always willing to lend a helping hand. I greatly appreciated him for allowing me to enjoy a break with my peers and boosting my morale.

As I went through the primary school challenges, I also enjoyed many benefits of education. I registered for extracurricular activities, including the school drama club, which helped me build self-confidence. Although I also participated in sports like athletics and high jumps, I wasn't particularly skilled in these sports. These activities helped me socialize with other students who shared similar interests.

At home, I juggled multiple responsibilities. In addition to attending classes, I had to assist my father in his small commercial endeavors, selling his handmade fans and fish in the local market. Despite its financial benefits to the family, I couldn't shake off feeling embarrassed when I had to sell fish on the streets, as my friends often teased me. Balancing schoolwork and home tasks was a challenging and frustrating experience. Still, I knew that dropping out of these two lives was not an option. I strived to pay attention to both, often studying at night, as I had no time in the afternoon.

On Saturdays, the regional weekly market day at Brikamaba, I often drove donkey carts to provide transport to market vendors. The familiar feeling of the rough rope reins in my hands and the gentle sway of the cart beneath me became a comforting routine. I helped local business owners transport their goods from one location to another, navigating the busy streets and bustling crowds. Now, I often remember those days with a sense of nostalgia. It was hard work, but I feel proud today that I started supporting my family at such an early age.

Nonetheless, I felt uncomfortable doing those after-school chores. Occasionally, I would bump into my friends and classmates when selling fish to their parents or transporting goods in the street. Some of these children mocked me with job titles like "fishmonger" or "donkey driver." I felt embarrassed to see them, even at school. I would sometimes hide when I saw them coming, especially from the children from Sapu Campus.

However, those difficult moments stoked my desire to want to do something else. I know that only my actions can help me achieve the desired changes. I realized that the petty business and farming helped my parents to afford uniforms, food in the house and sometimes lunch allowances for me.

In the end, my determination paid off. I completed primary school with good marks. My parents were proud of me, and I was proud of myself. These experiences taught me valuable lessons that I still carry with me. They helped me understand that there would be challenges as we strived to reach our goals. However, we can overcome obstacles with hard work, focus, and determination. These principles ultimately helped shape me into the person I am today.

CHAPTER FOUR

FIRST DROPPED OUT OF SCHOOL

In 1996, I completed my primary school education and was enrolled in Brikamaba Junior Secondary School. The school was brand new, and everything was still sparkling with the freshness of new beginnings. The lush green lawns were dotted with colorful flowers and tall trees, creating a serene and peaceful atmosphere. The school's exterior was painted in warm and inviting colors, making it impossible not to feel welcome as soon as I stepped foot on the premises.

As I walked with other students through the school halls for the first time, I couldn't help but admire the spacious and well-ventilated hall. The floors were polished to a shine and the desks and chairs were brand new. Everything was designed to make our learning experience as comfortable as possible.

The familiar government-supplied lunch and Friday pancakes were not available at this new school, but the beautiful campus more than made up for it. The serene atmosphere and state-of-the-art facilities were a refreshing change, and I felt a sense of excitement and opportunity as I settled into my new surroundings.

We were introduced to a new world of learning with Agricultural Science, Woodwork, Metalwork, French, and General Science classes. The familiar subjects like Math and English were broader than I had learned in primary school. As a boy from a farming community, I was particularly excited about the Agricultural Science class, as it connected with what I was familiar with from my experiences on the farm.

There were a few new students from the other primary schools in the Central River Region of the country. Despite my initial nervousness, I made new friends and formed connections with these diverse students.

The new school also came with its responsibilities. In the first term, the agriculture teacher gave each student different plants to grow on the school's premises. It was a difficult task because we had to water the plants twice a day, in the morning and evening. But despite the challenges, the students dutifully tended their plots, carefully pouring water and nutrients into the soil. The agricultural teacher was a strict taskmaster, constantly monitoring our progress to ensure we fulfilled our responsibilities. Neglecting our duties resulted in punishment, floggings ranging from on the palms to the back. The plants were our responsibility, and we took them seriously. Sometimes I had to return to the school in the evening to ensure the plants were watered before the teacher inspected them in the late evening.

My father was able to gather just enough money for my enrollment fees, uniform, and shoes, but textbooks and exercise books were a luxury we couldn't afford. Although the exercise books were made to contain one subject, I had to write two subjects in some books. Other than the issue of insufficient exercise books, the first term was smooth.

Nevertheless, during the second term, my father could not pay the school fees on time, and one day I was asked to leave the school until the fees were paid. It was my first embarrassing experience in junior school, as I was treated like a tenant who had refused to pay the landlord. At that time, the school authorities were very strict on tuition fee payments; failing to pay them resulted in them ejecting you from class. It was sad that there was no help from the government for the less financially privileged students who were willing to learn but could not pay their school fees.

Sometimes, the school management would wait until a week before the exam and send students home for failing to pay school fees. Fear of being sent home for unpaid fees gnawed at my mind, hindering my focus and draining my determination. The announcement of exam dates loomed like a dark cloud, casting a shadow over my studies and I only felt comfortable once my parents had paid the school fees.

A new school year started in September 1998, and I was promoted to grade eight. The school management assigned students to classes based on their seventh-grade results. All the students with the best results were put into grade eight circle, followed by eight-square, and the rest. I was happy to be in the best class, the eighth circle, with the best minds in the school. It was exciting and fulfilling. However, when I assessed it today, the school should have assigned us something other than individual performance. Some students in other classes may have felt judged and accepted their inability to score good results.

Nonetheless, as much as I enjoyed my new grade class during the first term, frustration cooked by poverty awaited me on the other side of the school term. My dad's long-standing eye issue, which gradually affected his vision, worsened. The doctors recommended that he undergo surgery as soon as possible, as it could lead to permanent blindness if not properly taken care of. Confusion and anxiety showed on every family member's face. My dad, a subsistence farmer and security man, could not afford enough for our basic needs, much less the ability to pay for surgeries. Therefore, it took him months before he could decide to go for surgery due to conflicting basic financial needs. There was no such thing as medical insurance for employees in our region. However, there was a man, in blessed memory, named Mr. Kasung Bayo, who later urged my father to undergo surgery. Kasung came from our village, was a distant cousin to my dad, and was a senior officer in Sapu. When my dad stayed home for over six months after the surgery, Kasung occasionally provided cash support to him.

While the weight of the financial and health situation was heavy on our shoulders, the impending deadline for the second-term tuition also knocked on our door. Every step felt uncertain as I struggled to make sense of the direction I was headed. It was as if I were searching for a needle in a haystack, the solution hidden among a jumbled mass of uncertainty.

I had received countless notices from the school authorities reminding me of my unpaid fees and looming expulsion. I had become adept at avoiding them, slipping out during the first class after the break time and sneaking back in for the second lesson. But one fateful day, fate caught up with me. The door creaked open, and Mr. Fatty, a senior teacher, stepped into the classroom. His eyes scanned the sea of faces as he moved to the teacher's table in front of the class.

"All those who have not paid their school fees should immediately stand up and leave the class." Mr. Fatty announced as he opened the folder containing the names of the school debtors.

A few students stepped out and peacefully left the class. I ignored his instruction as if my family had paid two years' tuition. I pretended to be reading, but all my other available senses were focused on the teacher. The fear of Mr. Fatty was the beginning of wisdom in the school. I still cannot explain where I got the conviction to ignore his instruction, but I suppose it was an embarrassment. He furiously looked into my eyes from a distance with the kind of look my mother would wear when she wants to give us instructions in public: a mix of concern, authority, and a hint of urgency. I knew Mr. Fatty wanted me to leave the class. So, I gave him my full attention.

"Ebrima Sawaneh." He called my name with anger. "Yes, sir." I responded in the best of manners as I became sober.

"Why are you wasting my time when you know you have not paid the school fee?" Mr. Fatty added as he moved in my direction. *I can't carry your family problem into my responsibilities*, he seemed to convey silently.

Sitting at my desk, I felt something was about to happen. My eyes flicked to Mr. Fatty, and I saw the anger simmering in his gaze. I knew what was coming—the familiar sting of his hand across my face. I quickly grabbed my bag and left through the back of the class, trying to put as much distance between us as possible. But he was relentless, moving towards me with purpose. The slap came like a freight train, and I barely dodged it. My heart pounding, I bolted out of the class and didn't stop running until I was outside the school. Rage and fear consumed me as I walked home.

I felt humiliated for something beyond my control. My mind raced with questions, and my heart was heavy with dread. I felt a whole gush of tears welling up in my eyes. Why did I have to be the one to bear the brunt of my parents' financial struggles? What will he do to me if I returned to school the next day without making any payment? These thoughts swirled like a storm in my mind, a constant reminder of poverty that plagued our community.

I arrived home, retreated to my room, and didn't engage in any conversations. As the day went on, I felt overwhelmed with sadness and helplessness. I agreed to return to school once my fees were paid in full. I had no choice.

CHAPTER FIVE

I BECAME A CARPENTER

The sun was setting, casting a golden glow over the small village as I sat alone under the veranda. My only company was the peeling old image of the drawing I had pasted on the walls. I stared blankly at it as in the deafening silence only broken by the occasional creak of our roof's old-corrugated iron sheet.

I had been sitting at home for more than two weeks, feeling the weight of hopelessness and despair pressing down on me. A single thought consumed my mind: the 150 dalasi I needed to pay my fees to resume school. I contacted my relatives for support, but none could help me. And the government, which I had once considered a solution, now seemed distant and uncaring. I felt trapped, with no way out of this endless cycle of desperation.

On a Monday morning, my mother said to me in a voice heavy with concern, "Kawsu, I think we should try something else. You've been home for over two weeks now, and we all know your dad's condition." My mother suggested that I learn a technical skill like carpentry or mechanics. She gave many examples of our villagers doing well as carpenters, drivers, and mechanics on the Sapu campus, where I had once dreamed of working as a clerk or an extension officer.

The idea of dropping out of school was painful and frustrating. I tried to imagine myself in workshops, but I could not. Instead, I pictured school activities, including classrooms, assemblies, and sports days. I sat wordlessly like a brick.

Mom leaned forward, searching my face for some crease of shared conviction. Tears began to build up in my eyes, but I faked peace and turned around, pretending to get a cup of water. The silence settled, its presence heavy.

I wanted to reject the suggestion but thought of my mother's pain. She was a strong and disciplined woman who wished the best for me. Her decision to recommend that I drop out of school must have been a bitter choice, like the prophet who took a knife and was ready to sacrifice his only son. I asked her to let me think about the idea, but I knew deep down that it was the only option.

If hard work were enough to bring wealth, my father and many others in our village would have been wealthy. My father had held a variety of jobs over the years. He had worked as a farmer, fisherman, and watchman. He was also skilled in making local fans and fishing nets. Sometimes we would spend the entire day on the island, and he would work as a watchman at night. However, despite his hard work and different trades, it only brought in a little income for our family.

Now that I am grown and have experience in parenting, I appreciate the role of my parents. Being a parent comes with a lot of responsibility. Your spouse, children, and sometimes extended families look up to you for guidance and support. No matter how hard you work, no one can take that responsibility off your shoulders. In corporate offices, we can resign from job functions or seek external support, but parents cannot resign or hire consultants.

I thought over my mother's proposal for a few days, then decided to drop out of school and learn carpentry in the city. I believed that the city would have carpenters with better tools, but really, the thought of staying home and seeing my friends go to school while I went to a workshop felt heartbreaking. I intended to stay at my grandmother's home in Bakoteh. However, I had to first visit Malick, my brother who stays with one of our uncles in Tallinding. Malick will take me to my grandmother's place.

My mother and I planned the trip together, as we were unsure if my father would agree. We were also concerned that the thought of my permanent drop out of school might further impair my father's health.

I was disappointed, but I knew I had to do something for a living. I believed that the decision could be a temporary setback and that I would return to school one day and complete my education. I hoped that it would not be too late.

We had a grand plan, but as expected, our pockets were as empty as a desert. I knew that the local police station in Brikamaba supported people in getting free transportation to the city via government vehicles or empty trucks from the hinterland. So, we agreed that on the following Saturday, I would go to the police station for help and then travel to the city.

I didn't sleep that Friday night. I lay on the bed and watched the hours tick by. Three A.M. Four. Five. I imagined how my father would discover that I was not around. The family would sit for lunch, and I would be absent. At dinner, the same thing would happen. He would be surprised I had not checked on him for a whole day. The next morning, he would ask my younger brother to check on me at a friend's compound. My brother would return and inform him that I had traveled or eloped to the city. Then, my mother would be questioned, and she would provide a better explanation.

At the crack of dawn, five a.m., I packed my best clothes in a nylon bag and quietly snuck out of the compound like a tenant eloping with unpaid rent. Outside, I was greeted by the village dogs, who barked at me. I stopped a few meters outside the village and prayed for a successful journey.

I walked alone through the inky darkness of the hill between Saruja and Brikamaba. The hill that had been the imaginary residence of wizards and demons. The moon, a mere sliver in the sky, provided the only light source as I made my way towards Brikamaba. But I had set out early that morning with nothing but a dream in my heart and a determination to do something that would change my family's life. My goal was to reach the city, learn the trade of carpentry, and lift my family out of poverty.

The journey was not easy, and I was forced to rely on the kindness of strangers. When I arrived at the Brikamaba garage, my heart was heavy with uncertainty about meeting a kind driver. I approached a truck driver and explained my predicament. "I want to reach the city to learn a trade, but I cannot afford the bus fare." The man listened patiently before directing me to the police station, where I pleaded my case.

As dawn broke and the sky turned a dull gray, the police officer finally secured a seat for me in a truck heading towards the city. The truck drove past the street that led to the school. My eyes darkened with sorrow as I glanced at the beautiful flowers we had planted at the school. I felt like I was leaving my dreams and everything familiar behind. The journey was long and arduous, as the driver took his time by frequently stopping along the way to pick up goods.

As the sun set and the sky settled to welcome the stars, my heart felt heavy with concern. I had last visited the city with my mother when I was a toddler, and I had no way of reaching out to my uncle. He was not aware I was coming. I didn't want anyone to change my mind or stop me from traveling to the city. But I was surprised that we had reached the city by that night. I closed my eyes in prayer, my mind half hopeful and half confused.

As the truck rumbled to our final stop after midnight, I couldn't help but feel a sense of unease wash over me. The driver asked if I knew my uncle's whereabouts, and I admitted that I had no idea where I was heading. I explained to him that my uncle is Kebba Sarjo Sawaneh, who lives in Tallinding and has a store in Serrekunda Market. The driver noticed my discomfort and kindly offered to take me to Serrekunda market the following morning.

I spent the night with strangers in a tiny boys' quarter in the driver's home in Tabokoto. The driver was like an angel; he watched over me throughout the journey and provided everything I needed, including food. As the sun rose the next day, we set off for the market. The driver asked around for anyone who knew my uncle, and by some stroke of luck, we were directed to a man who confirmed he knew where my uncle's shop was.

We were told to wait at a particular spot in the market, and soon enough, my uncle's kids arrived to take me to their home in Tallinding. It wasn't until the afternoon that Malick arrived home, and finally, I was reunited with someone familiar.

"Kawsu, how are you? What are you doing here? Are you not going to school?" Malick asked, with surprise written all over his face.

"I was sent out of the school as Daddy could not pay the second term's tuition," I replied as we shook hands. "I am here to learn carpentry."

Malick could do little about the financial challenges, as he was a student sponsored by his maternal uncle. However, I saw the disappointment and sadness on his long face throughout that evening.

We left for Bokoteh that evening through the bustling city of Serrekunda. The journey to my grandma Jonko's house was filled with a sense of hope and opportunity. I had heard tales of the wealth and prosperity of the city, and I knew my grandmother had a successful business. I couldn't wait to see what opportunities lay ahead—perhaps a chance to return to school or learn from skilled and educated carpenters.

The night was setting as we arrived at my grandmother's small home, and she was surprised to see me in the city when schools had not yet closed. She listened as I explained my situation and agreed that it was a good idea to learn a technical skill if school payments were a problem. However, she was concerned that she did not know anyone who could teach me carpentry. But she promised to ask her friends.

After spending a week with my grandmother, I discovered she was a petty trader and not as wealthy as I had imagined, but still financially better off than most people in our village. This discovery made me even more determined to acquire technical carpentry skills.

I scoured the town for a month, searching for a reputable carpentry workshop that would accept me as an apprentice. Similarly, I spent countless hours poring over old newspapers, my grandmother's go-to wrapping paper, searching for any scholarship opportunity. I could not find a suitable workshop or scholarship, but I remained determined and disciplined despite my disappointment. I kept pushing forward, focusing on one angle, and refused to give in to frustration or regret.

While I was in Kombo, my father's cousins, Kakuru and Kawsu Ceesay, visited him in the village. Kawsu Ceesay was based in Europe and came to the Gambia for a holiday. I learned that Kakuru asked about me, as they conversed. My father responded that I had traveled to the city. Kakuru disappointedly asked why I was not attending school, as he knew about my excellent results. Dad explained that I had gone there to learn carpentry skills because he could no longer afford my fees. Kawsu Ceesay was touched by my plight and asked my father to send someone to bring me back home. He promised to sponsor me until high school.

I was excited by the news that I would return to school. That week, my grandma gave me the travel fare, and I returned to the village.

Returning to school after missing more than a month of classes was daunting, but I was determined to catch up and pass my exams. The familiar faces of my classmates and teachers were a comfort, although I felt pressured as I borrowed notes and tried to make sense of the lessons I had missed.

I stayed up day and night reading my notes and revising old ones. When I could not afford a candle or kerosene in the room, I would pull the book to my nose and read under the moon.

With hard work, luck, and the prayers of my parents, I passed my second-term exams. The following term, I also had another good result, which led to my promotion to grade-nine-circle, the final class in junior secondary school.

Grade 9 was a year of newfound responsibility and respect. I was chosen to be a student councilor, which included inspecting classrooms and ensuring they were clean and organized. It was a lot of responsibility, but I felt proud to be in a position of leadership and to be able to make a positive impact on the school community. As student council members in the school, we were treated with a level of maturity and trust that we had not experienced before. The teachers and Parent Teacher Association (PTA) saw us as leaders and role models for the younger students. We were given the authority to enforce school rules, such as handing out light punishments to students who arrived late or were not dressed according to the school's dress code.

Being a school councilor also gave me my first formal leadership position, which was different from my informal leadership role in my boys' club in the village. Leading a diverse group of students was challenging but also very.

FINAL EXAMS. The air grew thick with tension as our final-year exams approached. First, each student was expected to choose a few elective subjects in addition to the core subjects. The girls, whose parents could afford it, often chose home economics, while most boys chose arts and crafts. Though it was an expensive course to study, requiring the purchase of fabrics for tie-dye and other materials, it was believed to be easier to pass than other practical subjects.

However, art was not my favorite subject; it was also too expensive. So, I did not choose arts and crafts due to a lack of finances to afford the requirements. Instead, I chose woodwork as one of my elective subjects. The woodwork choice offered me two benefits: the school paid the cost of all the materials needed to do the work, and the subject enabled me to learn practical skills that could be useful in case I couldn't proceed to grade 10 due to financial issues. Uncle Kawsu had promised to pay for my education, but I wasn't sure whether he would be able to sponsor me through high school. Hence, I always had a plan B. The woodwork subject allowed me to develop a skill set that would serve me well in the future, regardless of my financial situation.

Choosing woodwork as my elective subject of study had its own implications. The final product also belonged to the school, as the school provided all the materials for the practical work. I made an office tray with the guidance of our beloved teacher, Mr. Gomez. Though he is no longer with us, his teachings and guidance will always be in my memory.

In contrast, students in the arts and crafts class paid for their materials and could take their final art projects home. I watched my friends proudly show their beautiful tie-dyed garments adorned with intricate designs to their families as they excitedly told their families about the different techniques they had learned and the hard work they had put in to create these masterpieces. At that moment, I felt like an outsider, a lone pupil in a different school. I was often asked why I had no artwork to show, and I never knew how to answer. It reminded me of poverty, like a friend I didn't want to acknowledge, but everyone could see my relationship with it.

But I knew I had to keep my focus and strength and not let these feelings of inadequacy consume me. I never showed my parents any disappointment in not having the same resources as my peers. I kept to the wise words of my father, who once told me that we couldn't appreciate God for giving us what we had if we focused too much on what we didn't have. These words reminded me that we must look at our improvements over time.

As I reflect on my childhood, I am reminded of how fortunate I was to have had the opportunity to attend school. While countless children were denied this privilege or basic right, I was able to enter the classroom and learn. It was a gift that I never took for granted. I knew I had to seize the chance and make the most of it. The knowledge and skills I gained became my key to unlocking a brighter future. For this, I will always be grateful.

CHAPTER SIX

APRIL 10 & 11 – WHERE WERE YOU?

As the clock struck midnight on New Year's Eve, marking the beginning of a new millennium, the world erupted in cheers and fireworks. The new year brought a new story that I was eager to embrace. The year 2000 was my graduation year from junior to high school. With a grade nine certificate, I will become closer to my career aspirations, which kept changing as I learned new subjects.

In primary school, I aspired to work as a clerk at the Sapu agricultural campus. However, as a young student in grade 7, my career aspirations were shaped by my admiration for the news reporting of the late Kebba Dibba of Gambia Radio and Television Services (GRTS). Kebba's command of English and his reporting style left a lasting impression on me. But then my career dreams took a different turn as I fell in love with the hands-on approach of practical science classes in grade nine.

My favorite and best teacher in junior school was our science teacher, George Oris, a Nigerian who dedicated his time to educating young people in rural Gambia. He was not just a teacher but a mentor and a role model to many of us. His enthusiasm and passion for science made it one of my favorite subjects. Mr Oris also taught us physical education; his classes were always energetic and fun. His favorite slogan was "No leave, No transfer." That meant he would not take leave or be transferred to another school.

Mr Oris's teaching ignited my passion for electrical engineering especially as I saw its potential to solve our community's lack of electricity. Through our science classes, I understood the concepts of electric current flow and how it worked. I used this knowledge to wire my house using batteries, bulbs, and cables. The safety aspect of electrical engineering also caught my attention, as we were taught about the dangers of electricity and how it could be fatal if not handled properly.

The first term of the year was exciting as we celebrated the new year and the new millennium in different ways. On the other hand, the second term of Grade 9 was a traumatic time for many young Gambians. On the afternoon of the 10th of April 2000, I heard about the news of a strike on the national radio but never thought we would participate at my school. We were not used to strikes in the Gambia, at least not during my time in school. The students were protesting the brutality of security officers towards students.

On the 10th of April, the strike took place in the city. The following day, I prepared for school like any other day. But upon approaching the school from a distance, I saw students running from the school to the expressway, shouting that the soldiers were in the school, and they wanted to lock us in the classes. We joined the protest and threw stones at these armed soldiers without any idea that the soldiers would fire live bullets at a group of innocent teenagers. Small branches and leaves of trees fell in front of us, and we believed it was from the bullets the army fired in the air. A few meters from the incident site, we were told that someone was shot at the junction. With the fear of death approaching, many of us ran away from that path. I saw a man from our village who I believe came to rescue his children. The man urgently instructed us to go home while he proceeded to look for children from our village. Tragically, he was hit by a stray bullet as he approached the expressway. Fortunately, he survived after some months of recovery.

On the night of the second day of the protest, the soliders started to look for the students who had participated by searching the compound of the known students. Some of my classmates in the student council were arrested, especially those in Brikamaba and Dasilameh village and I learned the soldiers seriously tortured them. Luckily, I wasn't arrested or injured. However, I had nights of torture as my memory replayed the sound of bullets above our heads.

Our parents learned that the soldiers were also searching for the boys from our village who had actively participated in the strike. Therefore, the young boys were asked to hide. My mother insisted that I temporarily relocate to my aunt's house. She felt our home would be unsafe for me as everyone knew

I was a member of the student leadership. I finally relocated and restricted my movement because soldiers visit the village occasionally, intending to arrest any young boy found. It was a tough time for the community, especially for those families with teenage boys. As usual, the time was marked with prayers and well wishes.

Before the protest in April, we were a few weeks from the start of our final year external examination in junior school. The exam results would get us enrolled in high school. However, the strike trauma was affecting my studies. I could not focus on reading a single page for fear of being arrested by the soldiers.

After some weeks of staying home, I learned that school was resuming. I felt a sense of hesitation and fear. I imagined the soldiers storming into the school and arresting us for our participation in the strike. A feeling of dread seemed to cling to every thought.

The village parents consulted together and concluded that we could safely resume classes. We took our exams successfully without any issues, but the lingering shock of the strike undoubtedly impacted our results. The trauma was evident in our faces as we took our exams, our minds clouded by the memories of the violence we had experienced.

To this day, whenever I visit my old junior school, I can't help but recall the tragic events of April 10 and 11. The memories flood back like a bitter wave crashing against the shore: the sound of bullets ringing in my ears, the screams of students, and the fear that gripped my heart. It was a dark chapter in our lives that left a lasting impact on the lives of many young people, some of whom are now working in higher government offices and private institutions. I hope we work to ensure that such events are never repeated. The memory of those students who lost their lives and the trauma suffered by many of us will forever be engraved in my mind.

CHAPTER SEVEN

GRADE NINE RESULTS

Rain drummed on our tin-roofed house while I lay in bed, savoring its gentle rhythm. The joyful laughter of children playing in the rain reached my ears. It was another rainy season in the village. This was the time when farmers tirelessly tilled the soil and planted seeds, their hopes pinned on a bountiful harvest.

As the sun dipped below the horizon, village boys eagerly competed in a spirited football tournament known as "Nawetan." Their fans cheered and hollered in the evening breeze, filling the air with excitement.

While I couldn't help but feel a pang of nostalgia for the days when I too played and sang in the rain, my mind was preoccupied with a different concern. The looming exam results weighed heavily on my thoughts.

In the 9th grade, we had to choose a senior secondary school in the days leading up to the final external exams. I had two choices: Armitage High School and Nusrat High School.

Armitage was the school that many parents in our community liked. It was a boarding school located within our region, which meant students could visit the village every other weekend. But there was something I didn't like about it. At Armitage, the older students had a lot of power over the younger ones. They could give them challenging tasks and punishments for almost no reason. This made me uncomfortable.

On the other hand, Nusrat High School was farther from my home – in the city. But it had some good things going for it. The students at Nusrat did well in their exams. Plus, my older brother was in his second year at Nusrat, and he could help me if needed. However, Nusrat also has a high entry cut-off mark and often receives many applications nationwide. If Ivy League high schools were in the Gambia, Nusrat would have been a founding member.

In the end, I chose the famous Nusrat High School. However, Nusrat's high entry requirements made me concerned about whether my results would be enough to meet the cut-off.

Finally, the results were announced over the national radio. I felt uncertain as I wondered how I had performed. I made my way to the school, my heart beating fast. As I approached the principal's office, I felt a sense of nervousness wash over me. I received the slip of paper containing my results. I scanned it, looking past the individual subject scores to the aggregate.

My eyes fell upon the aggregate score: 28 (aggregate 6 being the highest possible score while 54 is the worst aggregate). My heartbeat increased. Happy beats! I couldn't contain my excitement as I stared at the number, feeling proud and accomplished. I had worked hard, and it had paid off.

My aggregate was above the national cut-off mark, and I had met the entry requirements for Nusrat. The thrill and accomplishment were overwhelming, and I couldn't wait to start this new chapter in my life.

Nusrat was known for consistently producing students who graduated with flying colors. Experienced teachers from Nigeria, Ghana, and Sierra Leone taught there, some of whom have published bestselling books. Interschool sports were the only national competitions that Nusrat High School couldn't seem to win, and I later realized that the reason was quite amusing. Instead of practicing on the field, the students would take their books and read them during the games. How could we expect to win when everyone focused on hitting the books instead of the ball?

My brother Malick told me there was no visible lifestyle difference at Nusrat because the rich and the poor students had to wear the same uniform: a crisp white shirt, long navy-blue pants, and white sports shoes. Like other missionary schools, Nusrat had strict rules, as the girls were not even allowed to wear certain earrings.

As I prepared to start my first year, although the school was known for its affordable fees, I knew there were still expenses to be covered. I needed a new uniform, shoes, and books, and my family's finances were tight. Our invisible friend poverty once again reminded me to think about the source of funding for basic materials and school fees. I knew it would be another rough ride before I settled in Nusrat.

However, the examination results gave me some hope. Anytime I looked at the results, a sense of triumph continued to wash over me. Despite numerous obstacles and challenges, I persevered and came out with one of the best results from our junior school. The excitement of my achievements boosted my morale and pushed me to work even harder. I was confident that poverty was becoming weaker as I progressed on my purposeful journey to pursue education.

Nonetheless, deep down, I couldn't shake off the nagging feeling that something was missing. I was hoping that Kawsu Ceesay, who had paid for my eighth grade and part of ninth grade, would somehow contribute. But there was little hope, as I hadn't been in touch with him for a long time. Nevertheless, I couldn't let that dampen my spirits, as I knew I had come too far to let anything hold me back.

A few days later, my father told me to prepare to travel to the city to attend high school. I would stay with my sister Jarra in Yundum, but my father was unsure who would pay for my education. He told me to meet Malick in Tallinding, who would help me contact Kawsu Ceesay.

As per customary practice in the village, my father called for a family meeting in the compound later that evening. Both men and women answered his call, and the children invited themselves. The objective was for the family elders to counsel me before I traveled to the city, to encourage, inspire, and advise me. The family gathered under a tent near my father's door. My father started with a prayer, and everyone shared their thoughts and wisdom. My late uncle Fulo told me, "As you go to the city, remember how we trained you, and you need to be focused on education like your elder brother, who has been there for years."

When called upon, my mom didn't say anything at first. "The men of the family have clearly said everything under the sun," she replied. Her voice was filled with sadness. She was probably thinking about how a mother could allow her teenage son to relocate to the city alone. A city is where you often find people from all walks of life. A place where some people succeeded in conquering poverty, but also a place where people failed to remember where they came from. She added that I should respect people, especially elders. My mother also reminded me of my early memories as she told me to focus on education. She said my health condition may not permit me to do hard physical labor. In primary school, I always got sick, especially during the summer when malaria is often rampant in rural areas. Hence, I should continue to focus on education. "For all the things you have been through, if you focus on education, you will surely make it through with enough determination." She continued but couldn't hold back her tears anymore.

Eighteen years later, when I watched the speech of Dananjaya Hettiarachchi, the 2014 World Champion of Public Speaking Toastmasters, I remembered my mother's tears. Dananjaya said mothers cry for three reasons: "tears of joy, tears of sorrow, and tears of shame."

My mother's tears were more tears of joy than tears of sorrow. She had seen my growth from being a baby to a focused boy, but she knew that my relocation to the city would bring distance and an unknown destination. When sons leave for the city, they often settle there and become tourists in the village. Some come for short holidays, while others never return. But I knew that my mother's tears were not only of sadness but also of happiness and pride as she saw me pursuing my dreams and aspirations of going to school.

The family meeting that evening was solemn, and I knew it was a momentous occasion, a rite of passage. I felt responsible for living up to their expectations of bringing about change in the family. I spent half the night thinking about the words of advice from the elders. In the end, I concluded that everyone was saying the same thing: to maintain family values and to focus on education. Their words reminded me to stay true to my roots and be proud of where I came from, no matter where life takes me.

PART TWO

one didn't need to know someone to extend kindness to them; the kindness shown by parents can have a lasting impact on their children elsewhere.

CHAPTER EIGHT

IT TAKE A VILLAGE TO EDUCATE A CHILD

The usual cry of hens crowing filled the air and the nearby mosque announced the call to the Fajr prayer. Soon after, the first light of dawn approached, signaling the start of a new day.

I woke up, took a bath, and performed my morning prayers. I then sat down for a special breakfast made by my mother: peanuts pounded with rice. As I ate, I knew that would be my last breakfast with my family for a while. I was ready to leave for the city, pursue knowledge, and make a better life for my family.

The family sat down in the middle of the compound and offered their prayers and best wishes for me. As they told me their goodbyes, I felt a mix of emotions. I felt sad that I was leaving my family and friends behind in the village. I felt sad that I would now be a tourist in the village, only visiting occasionally. But on the other hand, I was excited to be on my way to pursue knowledge, a mission that was a core part of the changes we were all hoping for.

This time, I took a bus from the Brikamaba bus station to Yundum. After hours of travel, I finally arrived in Yundum around 3 p.m. I spent the night with my sister's family. The next day, I visited Malick in Tallinding to discuss my admission and payment options. However, to my dismay, Malick informed me that he had no idea where my sponsor was. I was devastated and felt that I might never be able to attend high school. But Malick suggested we visit Kemo Ceesay, Kawsu's younger brother, who lived in the same city.

In the evening, we walked to Kemo's house. Malick explained the situation and asked if Kawsu might have discussed my sponsorship with Kemo. Kemo had never met me before but was friendly and asked to see my results. After looking at them, he said we should get the bill from the school while he tried contacting Kawsu about the school fee payment.

I was still worried but felt much better since meeting Kemo. Malick and I went to the school to pick up information about the school requirements, including fees and uniforms and presented the school fee bill to Kemo. He maintained that Kawsu had not contacted him since our last visit.

Nevertheless, he offered to support paying the first-term school fee to enable me to start classes on time while we waited for Kawsu. I felt elated, excited, and alive. It was a defining moment as the school fee matter was resolved and I was ready to start other admission procedures into the prestigious Nusrat

High School. The joy in my heart was more significant than the results that got me admitted to Nusrat.

REGISTRATION. When I went to register for school, I discovered the requirement to provide a birth certificate and my junior secondary results. The problem was that I had never seen my birth certificate, and no one knew my exact date of birth. Even my vaccination card, which could have helped, was lost in a fire, as my mother once told me. My parents would only refer to an event instead of a date. My father said I was born when the Jahal-Pacharr rice project was inaugurated. So, we could not even rely on the village records to determine my birth date.

After a full day of worrying, our late uncle Kebba Sarjo came up with a solution. He suggested that I use his eldest son's birth certificate. His son and I were born around the same time, so it was a perfect match. His son's name was also Ebrima, so we had the same name and a similar birth period. Problem solved.

After the registration formalities, the uniforms, textbooks, and other materials became the most critical items I needed to start school like other students. I acquired some old uniforms from a family friend and a cousin, Mama Bayo Junior, the son of the late Alhagie Alieu Bayo, who was in grade eleven at Nusrat High School. My elder sister also gave me money from her petty trade, which I used to purchase notebooks. I could not afford to buy even a single textbook. One of the reasons I had chosen to study commerce in high school was to enable me to use my older brother's old books. Yaya Fatty, an uncle who visited the city, also gave me about 200 dalasis, which I used to buy a pair of shoes. Like a bird building its nest, I finally acquired all the minimum materials and money needed to start school.

All these joint efforts that helped me start high school classes reminded me of the saying that it takes a village to raise a child. Yes, I was born into the Sawaneh family, but I am a son of the Saruja village. The Son of the Gambia. The Son of Africa. Unknown to each of these people, they have contributed something that might be small to them but was significant to me; a contribution that helped me get one step closer to my mission of purposeful education and to break barriers.

Although Kemo had settled the first term's school tuition, there was still some uncertainty about my ability to continue my education as he did not promise to sponsor the entire year. However, during our discussions, Malick shared a piece of information with me about how I could secure a scholarship. He told me that Nusrat offered a one-year scholarship to students who achieved the overall first position in their class.

I was initially excited about the possibility of securing a scholarship, but as I thought about it more, self-doubt crept in. Coming from a rural junior school with an aggregate of 28, attending Nusrat Senior Secondary School in the city and achieving the first position seemed like Tom Cruise's mission impossible. Nusrat's reputation for having brilliant students and a competitive academic environment was known throughout the country. How could I, the boy from the village with a poor educational foundation, even consider the possibility of a first position in Nusrat? These self-doubts clouded my mind for days. However, the more I doubted myself, the more I decided I would study hard to avoid taking the last position in the class full of brilliant students from top schools in the city. The determination to succeed in exams to prevent the embarrassment of last position continued to sit heavy on my shoulders until the first-term results were announced.

CHAPTER NINE

I WILL NOT TAKE LAST IN THIS CLASS

I woke up early in the morning on my first day of high school. I took a quick shower and donned my crisp new uniform, feeling like a new person. My heart pounded with excitement. As I rushed to catch the school bus, I couldn't help but feel a sense of nervous anticipation. This was my first time riding on a school bus, and I was eager to see what it was like.

I climbed aboard, where a sea of unfamiliar faces greeted me. The bus was packed with students from Brikama and the surrounding communities, all jostling for space. I squeezed through the crowd, feeling out of place among all the older teenagers. But as the bus started to move, the energy in the air became palpable as everyone chattered excitedly, laughing, and joking as we drove to school.

The school bus wound its way through the streets, stopping to pick up and drop off students from different schools and communities. Finally, we arrived at a bus stop in Tallinding.

The bus stop where I and other Nusrat students disembarked. After more than a kilometer of walking from the bus station to the school premises in Bundung, I was relieved that we made it to school on time.

I walked into the classroom and scanned it for the perfect seat. I finally settled on the middle row, deliberately avoiding the back, where I knew the troublemakers usually sat, and the front row, which the teacher could call upon to answer questions.

As I was getting comfortable, the bell rang, signaling the start of assembly. I quickly gathered my things and went to the assembly ground. The assembly ground was already buzzing with activity when I arrived. Students were talking and laughing, and the air was filled with excitement. I found a spot to stand and waited for the assembly to begin.

The assembly started with a reading of the Hadith of the day. Then, the press club team gave a brief update on the latest news. Finally, the principal welcomed everyone to the school, especially the grade 10 students. I listened attentively, but my mind was already racing ahead for the rest of the day.

When we returned from assembly and were about to take our seats, a medium-height, fair-complexioned gentleman walked into our class. The entire class fell silent as he made his way to the front of the room.

"Good morning, class; welcome to the Nusrat Senior Secondary School," he said, his voice friendly and clear. "My name is Martin Tucker, the form teacher of this class, Grade 10 Commerce One. I am also your math teacher."

We all greeted him in unison. He continued introducing himself, sharing his background and experience. I could see the spark in his eyes—I could tell that he loved teaching and was passionate about mathematics.

Mr. Tucker asked us to introduce ourselves by stating our names and the names of our previous schools. Listening to my classmates, I realized I could be the only one from a rural school. Most of my classmates were from nicely named schools in the city, like LK and Botroop.

I noticed the looks of surprise and curiosity on the faces of some classmates when they heard my school's name. I almost heard their thoughts: "Which school is this boy coming from?" Some students even asked me later which region my school was located in.

Aside from the name of my school, other factors made me feel like I didn't fit in. Being less privileged, I noticed that almost every student in my class had complete textbooks, mathematical set box and other supplies, while I struggled to make do with what I had. This made me feel worried and somewhat humbled.

However, Mr. Tucker must have noticed my reaction because his inspiring words afterwards touched my soul. He spoke about how Nusrat was a great school that had produced some of the brightest minds in the country and reminded us that we were chosen from hundreds of students who applied to the school. He emphasized that it didn't matter where we came from; we had the potential to achieve greatness if we put in the effort.

Those words stayed with me, and I became even more determined to study hard and avoid falling behind my classmates. Coming from a rural school, I knew I might have to work harder than my classmates to prove myself and overcome knowledge gaps. I was determined to put in the extra effort required to bridge any potential asymmetry in information and show that I was just as capable as anyone else in my class. And I was ready to do just that.

From that first day onward, every day was a reason for me to prepare for the exams. I revised the notes I had taken on every topic and subject we covered in class each day before going to bed. I was determined to make the most of my time at this school and do well in all my subjects. This learning method gave me a deeper understanding of the class notes, and I could participate more actively in class discussions and ask more insightful questions.

Two months into the first term, I relocated to Tallinding to stay with Malick in our uncle's compound. The relocation became a turning point that allowed me to read and revise my notes every day, at any time. Malick was in Year 12 and had already gone through the same class and most of the subjects that I was reading in Grade 10. I started to read Malick's Grade 10 notes ahead of the class, which gave me an advantage over many of my classmates.

The act of daily revision and reading ahead of the class teacher and students became the most crucial game-changer for me in the school. It fed my confidence and led to my active participation in class. In some instances, I was the only student who could correctly answer specific questions in class or get homework right.

On the first examination day, I walked into the hall with an air of quiet and shyness on the outside, but inside, I felt a strong sense of confidence. As I scanned the examination questions, I felt relieved, as they were not as difficult as I had anticipated. Though the dream of getting a scholarship flashed in my mind, my confidence in achieving it was still low. Avoiding the last position was more important for me.

Soon after came the first December of the new millennium, and like many others, people were busy planning for festive celebrations, Christian and Muslim alike. But the only thing on my mind was our first-term examination results, which would be released on the school's closing day, mid-December.

THE LAST DAY OF THE TERM. When I entered the classroom, there was no teacher present. Most of the other students were engaged in lively discussions at their desks, causing a commotion throughout the room. Meanwhile, my heart was filled with eager anticipation. As the morning progressed, Mr. Tucker finally arrived in the classroom.

"Please, who is Ebrima Sawaneh?" Mr. Tucker asked as he stood at the class entrance with empty hands. Of course, he did not pronounce my name correctly. There was total silence in the class. I looked to my left and right and decided not to answer for two reasons. First, there was a Ebrima Suwaneh (take note of the second name spelling) in my class. Secondly, I was curious whether it was good or bad news. Then, one of the students asked Mr. Tucker to clarify which Ebrima he was referring to, as we had two students with similar surnames.

"I mean Ebrima B. Sawaneh," Mr. Tucker repeated, spelling my surname clearly and using my initials. I lifted my hand and stood up, though my increased heartbeat gave me mixed feelings that something was wrong. Mr. Tucker thanked me and left the class without any further information. I sat down, feeling the weight of everyone's eyes. I became confused and quiet.

About an hour later, Mr. Tucker returned to the class with an envelope that contained our first-term results. Standing before the class, he called every student to collect their results except me.

"Ebrima Sawaneh," he now called me. Before he gave me my results, he asked me to stand next to him. Still, my mind could not guess what I had done.

"Although the overall performances are excellent, Ebrima here got the best result in the class for this term," Mr. Tucker announced.

I felt a sense of relief, but it was a relief that came with a fast heartbeat, as if I had avoided some unwanted outcome. I felt amazed as my classmates clapped at me. My face relaxed, and my cheeks raised in a smile. Despite being from an unknown rural school and small village, I took the first position in a class in Nusrat. As my lips curled upwards, my cheeks gracefully ascended, forming the contours of a radiant smile that seemed to illuminate the very essence of my being. In that transformative instant, the knots of doubt and uncertainty deeply rooted in me began to unravel, leaving a canvas of triumph and transcendence.

Some of my classmates were happy and congratulated me. But I could see disappointment etched on the faces of a few. One of the students even jokingly said it was the last time I would take the first position in the class. However, for me, clinching the first position felt akin to embodying the essence of the lion and gazelle tale from an African proverb.

Every morning in Africa, a gazelle wakes up. It knows it must run faster than the fastest lion, or it will be killed. Every morning, a lion wakes up. It knows it must outrun the slowest gazelle, or it will starve to death. It doesn't matter whether you are a lion or a gazelle: when the sun comes up, you'd better be running.

I had kept to my intense study like a lion and gazelle with a purpose to survive. The first position was like a spark that ignited a flame within me, giving me confidence that I could win the Nusrat Jehan Award Scholarship. The scholarship was a critical backup to funding my high school education in case Uncle Kemo or Kawsu could not support me. I felt I would have to either maintain the first position or drop out of school.

With the burning desire and elated confidence to fight for the scholarship, I intensified my everyday studies like I was preparing for my final year in high school. I created the title "MANSA" for myself during this time. In the Mandinka tribe, MANSA means "king." However, my MANSA stands for "**M**anagement as an **A**ttitude of a **N**imble **S**tudent in his **A**ctivities." I created study timetables and ensured maximum use of the available hours, especially during the day.

During the holiday, I visited Uncle Kemo to show him the results. He was in an ecstasy of delight and was proud of me. He was so excited and informed me that he would continue to pay my school fees. The news that Uncle Kemo would pay the school fees was like a ray of sunshine on a cloudy day. It was a moment of joy and gratitude, like a little bird finally finding its way home. It was a moment when God answered the prayers. I spent the whole Christmas holiday pouring over my brother's notes and familiarizing myself with the material the class would cover when the school opened.

JANUARY 2001, the beginning of a new year and the second term in school. I religiously maintained my daily study routine and continued to read ahead of the class. When the second-term results came out, I took the first position. Many classmates continued trying to replace me in the top seat, but I was determined to maintain my position. I was like a fortress, unyielding and unshakable in my resolve to get the scholarship. My name was again declared for the first position when the third-term results were announced. These results officially make me the overall best student in the Commerce One class for the academic year 2000-2001.

Soon after, the school announced the date of its annual speech and award ceremony, a momentous event for any school. It was an occasion where the final-year students and the best of the ongoing students were recognized with awards in front of parents and other dignitaries. My name was shortlisted as the only recipient from our class.

AWARD CEREMONY DAY. The sun rose over the horizon as I emerged from my slumber, greeted by a wave of euphoria and a hint of trepidation. I meticulously smoothed out the wrinkles in my crisp school uniform and aligned each button with precision. Striding towards the school, I felt like a dignitary, my heart pounding with exhilaration as the ceremony drew near.

As I took my seat among the award recipients, I felt a sense of elation. The special sitting area assigned to us was a mere stone's throw away from the esteemed teachers and important guests. I felt like a VIP among the true elite.

I opened the official program brochure, and my eyes were drawn to my name among the many listed on its pages. It was a tangible reminder of the countless hours of hard work and dedication that had led me to this moment. I feel an overwhelming sense of pride.

As the ceremony reached its climax, the air was filled with anticipation as the awards were about to be presented. I heard my name called out, announcing me as the best student from Commerce One. With a sense of purpose, I gracefully made my way to the stage, my steps steady and sure. I felt a sense of pride and accomplishment as I stood before the audience. "*A village boy who had once struggled to pay school fees is now being recognized for his achievements.*" I was thinking.

It was an uplifting feeling. I felt like an artist whose design was beginning to take shape. I received a cash voucher and a certificate. It was like receiving my first salary, taking the burden off my parents' shoulders. The award's impact was immeasurable. It provided me with financial support and brought hope to other students from the rural community. I could feel the excitement of my friends who attended the same junior school as me. It symbolized hope that, despite coming from a village, we too, could achieve greatness.

A week after the award ceremony, I traveled to my village to spend the summer with my parents. In a farming community, the summer session is the most critical time when every parent wishes their son or daughter to be with them to help with the cultivation. I spent over two months working on my parents' farms, tending to the crops. But it was not just a chore for me. It was an opportunity to seek blessings and connect with my home.

My late grandfather, Fakebba Fatty, used to tell me that the best prayers always come from parents because their intentions are pure. He would say, "You can visit all the marabouts and imams, but none of them will pray that you are better than them or their children." Only parents pray for their children and say, "May your life be better than mine." However, Grandpa would remind me that we must earn those prayers by taking some burdens off our parents' shoulders.

As a student, my only earning ability was to go to the farms and offer my services to the family. Without a word, I knew my parents were praying day and night, in the mosque and at home, for a prosperous future for me.

As the sun set on the final day of my summer holiday, I prepared to return to the bustling metropolis. My mother had spent the previous day meticulously pounding a mixture of peanuts and rice, enough to provide nourishment for my meals for the next three months.

On the morning of my departure, the family gathered in front of my father's house one more time to offer me prayers and best wishes for my journey. This time, my mother did not shed a tear. Perhaps she believed I had grown into a capable young man, having successfully navigated my first year in the city.

CHAPTER TEN

COLLABORATION IS BETTER THAN COMPETITION

The summer ended, seeming to have been evaporated by its own heat. We prepared to resume another academic year. As I set foot on the grounds of Nusrat, a wave of renewed confidence and energy swept through me. The summer break had been a time of tireless dedication and hard work. I had spent my days toiling in the fields at the farm and my nights poring over the upcoming term's curriculum, all with the single-minded goal of maintaining my position at the top of the class.

In Grade 10, I had felt isolated and excluded, especially among the boys. As a result, during break time, I often left my class and spent time with friends from the same junior school who were in science 2. I found solace in their company and would often stay there until the bell rang to announce the end of the break.

However, as the new term of 11th grade began, I noticed a shift in my social dynamics. I made new friends, particularly among my female classmates. They started to approach me for support and guidance. I began to lead revision sessions with these girls during breaks or when one of our regular lesson teachers was absent.

I kept up with my usual study routine. But it was not always easy. I lived in my uncle's compound, a home to many other high school students like me. With so many young people around at night, finding a quiet place to focus on my studies was challenging. I started going to the library after school to read and stay there until late evening.

THE FIRST TERM RESULT. It was another end of the term, and we had just finished the first term exams of grade 11. The results were announced, and as expected, I emerged victorious, again placing my name at the top of the class.

The second term brought with it a change in the winds. Some of the boys in my class began to join the discussions I often had with the girls. The boys may have recognized that, while I may have claimed the first seat in class with fierce determination, I was also eager to share my knowledge and help others along the way. As the term progressed, we grew to know each other better, bonding over our shared love of learning and our desire to make the most of our school memories.

My passion for teaching mathematics and financial accounting had been noticed by my peers, who often turned to me for assistance. It wasn't long before the teachers noticed my willingness to help. On days when the teachers were absent or occupied, they entrusted me to lead discussions on topics I understood.

My willingness to share my knowledge and help others understand these subjects had a ripple effect throughout the class. Other students began to take a keen interest in other subjects, like economics and geography. I felt a sense of pride, knowing I had played a small part in inspiring their curiosity.

Nusrat was, and still is, one of the most highly regarded schools in the Gambia. It is known for fostering a culture of fierce competition among its students. But as I progressed through my education there, I realized that being in a school was not about competition but rather collaboration among my peers. While I may have been the best student in my class, I was not necessarily the best in every subject. My English could have been better.

We shifted our mindset and silently decided that cooperation worked better than competition. We understood that working together as a group made learning easier for all of us, with less chance of failure among our classmates. We focused on sharing our strengths and helping one another overcome our weaknesses. The result was a more harmonious and productive learning environment where everyone could achieve their best.

At some point, we started to welcome students from other commerce classes as well as art students. Our group quickly grew in popularity and numbers, with students from other schools joining us.

Brainstorming and discussing various topics became regular occurrences in our study group. It was our unique way of learning, where we all contributed our ideas and perspectives. As we spent more time together, we became better students and friends. Even 20 years after our high school graduation, I am still in touch with some classmates. Collaboration is genuinely better than competition.

Nonetheless, high school was another rough journey throughout the ride. Most days, I could not afford to eat at the school canteen, as times were tough. There was a food court under the sprawling branches of trees adjacent to the school library, a familiar sight to most Nusrat students. However, my visits to the food court were like those of a tourist who comes once in a blue moon. The food vendors who might remember me are the petty roasted groundnut sellers who sit outside the school gate and there were days when I could not afford to buy roasted groundnuts for myself.

During one of my examinations, my pen grew heavy as I stared at the blank paper before me, trying to ignore the gnawing hunger in my stomach. The minutes of the clock ticked by, the hands moving with maddening slowness. I could hear the muffled sounds of my classmates scribbling away, their pens scratching against the paper. But all I could focus on was the empty feeling in my stomach and how it seemed to twist and knot in protest.

I tried to push the feeling aside to concentrate on the questions before me. But it was a constant battle, with my brain and stomach vying for attention. The stomach would remind me that it had been hours since I had last eaten, while the brain begged for silence to recall the information, as we were in an exam hall.

I didn't let it get to me, however. I knew I had to focus on the task and push through the hunger and distraction. I took a deep breath and let my eyes wander, taking in the hustle in the exam hall. I wrote until my hand ached, and the bell rang for us to stop.

And at that moment, I knew that hunger can be a distraction to change from poverty to freedom. When people don't have enough to eat, it can be tough for them to focus on improving their lives. But I saw myself as someone on a breakthrough mission, and education, as I concluded, was the best way to break free from poverty.

CHAPTER ELEVEN

FINAL YEAR IN HIGH SCHOOL

Although Nusrat High School is a Muslim missionary school, it admits non-Muslim students too. The school operates Mondays through Thursdays, and Saturdays. It is closed on Friday and Sunday. I believe this was done so Muslims could attend their Jumma prayers on Fridays and Christians could attend churches on Sundays. Our weekends were not enjoyable because we had to attend classes on Saturdays. I found it a bit weird, as we also had an assembly every day where we sometimes only listened to news from the Press Club and read the Hadith of the day.

Beyond the excellent teachers, Nusrat provided strong support to its students. One of these was summer classes for students moving into their final year, which helped ensure they were well-prepared for their exams. The school also occasionally organized night classes to help students cover the syllabus. Some of these classes were led by the school principal, Karamo

S Bojang, an experienced mathematician. Mr. Bojang and I had one thing in common: we were both excellent in mathematics, but our English language skills could have been better.

Many students traveled for holidays as the school year ended and summer break began. However, as a Grade 11 student who would be sitting for the final high school examination the following year, I had to stay for summer revision classes. Unlike internal school exams, the final high school examination is set and marked by an independent external regional body, the West African Examination Council (WAEC). Every school must cover the approved syllabus to increase their students' success rate on the exam.

The final year's exams are known to be difficult and important for many purposes. The results are a key determinant of admission into local and international colleges and universities, and even for job applications in The Gambia. Additionally, doing well in high school final exam could help me obtain scholarships to the University of The Gambia. Nonetheless, the pressure of the uncertainty of the exams always made me feel as though my studies were insufficient. Hence, I doubled my study efforts during my final year of high school.

Each day, when the bell signaling the end of the school day rang out, I would buy a small bag of roasted groundnuts and savor the salty taste as I crunched on the delicious snack. With a satisfied stomach, I would go to the library, my sanctuary of knowledge and learning. As I read, the hours flew by while the sun slowly set outside the window. Before I knew it, it would be 5 p.m., and I would reluctantly close the book.

It was sometimes challenging at home to find a quiet place to read. Sometimes I couldn't afford a candle to light my way, and other times my roommates were too busy to allow me a peaceful reading session.

Towards the end of 2002, I had the chance to relocate to the compound of the late Sorrie Bayo in Tallinding, where Malick was residing. The compound was tranquil, consisting of only two rooms. This atmosphere allowed me to read late at night, but I faced the constant challenge of funding the cost of candles.

As the final year exams drew near, I found myself with less and less time during the day to study. The pressure of the upcoming exams weighed on me like a heavy burden. I knew that I had to make the most of every available moment if I wanted to succeed.

So, I began to take advantage of the longer nights by studying at the Jammeh Foundation with my friend Kebba S. Camara. We would leave our homes around 10 p.m. and then spend hours poring over our books and notes, trying to absorb as much information as possible. The quiet night and the study-friendly environment helped us focus and retain most of our notes. We would take short breaks to pray and return home after 5 a.m.

I would be starving for sleep by the time I reached home. But still, I would wake up early to prepare for school. My hair was often unkempt and overgrown, as I needed to find the time to trim it. Some days, I would even arrive at school late.

Despite my busy schedule, I pushed through and continued to work hard.

As time passed, my classmates and I realized our paths were diverging. Some of us planned to enroll at the University of the Gambia, while others aimed to attend universities in foreign countries like the United States and the United Kingdom. The pressure was high to get good results, as everyone wanted to ensure they could achieve their goals.

I set my sights on the University of the Gambia, as I would have needed more support to attend a foreign university. It wasn't that I didn't want to study abroad, but I had to consider the financial realities of my family and the cost of attending even the University of Gambia. I tried not to overthink the future and instead focused on my studies, knowing that earning a scholarship or national award would help with the expenses.

The biggest obstacle I faced was the English language. I wasn't solid in it and wished all subjects were calculations instead. But I was fortunate that I had teachers with a good command of the English language, and their support helped me improve.

I was always drawn to people in school who spoke English fluently, particularly the students who would read the morning announcements from the art classes. I needed help to study and understand English, maybe because I was preoccupied with mathematics and accounting.

I realized that my foundational education also played a significant role in my struggles with the English language. I didn't attend nursery school, and I don't recall having learned the sounds of the English alphabet in primary school. Despite these challenges, I am grateful I was able to attend school.

Finally, it was time for the examination. As I walked into the exam hall, I could feel my heart pounding. I had spent the last three years of high school studying and preparing for this moment, and now it was time to put all that knowledge to the test. I tried to push away the feeling of anxiety and focus on the task at hand.

As I sat down and began the first exam paper, I easily focused and answered most of the questions. Completing each exam paper was a small victory and felt like weightlifting off my shoulders.

As I walked out of the hall on the last day of the exam, a sense of relief washed over me. I had done it. I had put my hard work to the test and completed all the exam papers. I felt like I could finally breathe again.

PARTY TIME. After the last exam papers, our study group organized a beach party to celebrate our hard work and the end of high school. It was a relaxing and memorable event, especially compared to when we had first met in Grade 10. As the night sky descended upon the sea, we bid farewell to one another with hugs and promises to keep in touch. The music, laughter, and chatter that had filled the air all evening slowly dissipated, leaving behind a sense of nostalgia and longing. But just as we packed our bags, Tida Drammeh, one of my closest classmates, called for everyone's attention. With a gentle smile, she spoke about how we had all grown from strangers in grade

10 to friends in grade 12, united by our shared struggles and triumphs. As she spoke, I felt a swell of emotion rise within me as memories of all the days we'd spent studying together and all the laughter we'd shared flooded my mind.

And then she turned to me, her gaze locking onto mine. She said I deserved special recognition for being a good friend and brother to everyone in our study group who had always been willing to share knowledge with others. My heart skipped a beat as I realized what was happening. Tida then pulled out a gift from a bag, which she presented to me on behalf of the whole group.

The gift was wrapped in shiny silver paper and tied with a ribbon. I could feel the eyes of my friends upon me as I carefully undid the ribbon and peeled back the wrapping. Inside, I found a beautiful shirt, the fabric soft to the touch. I was overcome with emotion and couldn't find the words to express my gratitude. My other classmates also gave speeches about me and how helpful I had been to them. I was humbled by their kind words and felt a sense of warmth spread through my chest.

The gift was a thoughtful and meaningful gesture that I would treasure forever. It reminded me that the bonds we form in life truly matter and that the people we share our journey with make it all worthwhile.

CHAPTER TWELVE

IT WAS TIME TO HARVEST

A week after the group party, I traveled to my village. I had two reasons for leaving the city: first, unlike most of my friends, I couldn't afford to enroll in any new courses until the high school results were released. Second, I wanted to help my parents on the farm during the summer harvest.

AT THE FARM. The sun beat down on my skin as I walked through the fields, the heat radiating off the dry earth. The short, green stalks of rice swayed gently in the breeze, their plump heads heavy with grains. The smell of fresh grasses and the sound of crickets singing in the fields were like a soothing balm to my soul. The logged memories hit me, my childhood memories of playing in the muddy puddles, swimming in the irrigation canals, and throwing fishing hooks. This field had been my playground as a child, and now I was returning to it as a young adult. This land, this field, and this community were all a part of who I was, and I felt grateful.

The party, the school, and the exams seemed so far away now as I stood there, looking out over the rice fields. I knew that this was where I belonged and that this was where I would always call "the beginning". I am here to harvest the rice field, but first, I must protect the rice from hungry birds.

The days were spent in a peaceful yet focused manner. The rice fields were alive with activities as the boys and I moved through them purposefully while the misty morning light gave way to the bright sun, and the gentle sway of the rice stalks became a dance in the breeze. Our mission was clear: to protect the rice from the birds that would come to feast on it.

As we stood, our eyes scanned the sky, searching for any sign of movement that would signify the presence of birds. We were like hunters, stalking our prey with stealth and precision. Our slingshots were our weapons, and we were experts in their use.

When we spotted a flock of birds circling overhead, we raised our slingshots and aimed. With a swift flick of the wrist, a pebble was launched into the sky, soaring towards the birds. The birds scattered in a panicked frenzy, their wings flapping wildly as they tried to escape. The sound of whistling pebbles and the panicked cries of birds filled the air as they fled for safety.

Our slingshots were our trusty tools, protecting our delicate rice crops. We felt satisfied with each flock of birds we scared away, knowing our efforts would ensure a bountiful harvest for our families.

IT WAS TIME TO HARVEST

As the sun gets hotter, the birds vanish. We rest under tents, watchful for any remaining birds. In the evening, the battle goes on till sunset. We head back to the village, slingshots ready for tomorrow.

After a month of sling-throwing operations, I joined forces with my friends to harvest the rice fields. We formed a network to pool our resources and work together to get the job done. We left for the farm early in the mornings before the sun rose to make the most of the cool air. The dew still clung to the tall green stalks of rice, glistening in the rising sun's light. The fields stretched out before us, a seemingly endless expanse of yellow and green.

The sun slowly climbed higher in the sky, bearing down on us. The work was hard; the stalks of rice were heavy in our hands as we cut them down and bundled them into neat piles. But it was also rewarding as we watched the fields slowly change from green to golden.

As the sun set, casting a warm orange glow over the fields, we headed back home, tired but content. The harvest days were long and hard, but also fulfilling. It was the last time I worked heavily on our family farm, the last time I would work closely with my father in the farm operations.

The rice field was harvested and brought to the village, and the community was filled with joy. The field had a bountiful harvest that year, and everyone was happy to be able to eat the grown-in-Saruja rice once more. But for me, there was still an important personal harvest: I was waiting for the results of my final high school examination.

Although I had received excellent results from grade 10 to the final mock examination of grade 12, the fear of failing some subjects, like English, still loomed in my mind. I had always struggled with the language, and the thought of not passing it, even with all my hard work, was daunting.

As the days passed, the results were finally released. I couldn't wait to return to the city to collect my exam results. I arrived in the evening but was eager to visit the school the following day.

I held my breath as I received a piece of paper from the vice principal. I scanned the page, looking for my name and then the English language grade. And there it was - a passing grade of C - better than I had expected. Overall, I achieved 5 As, 2 Bs, and 1 C. The Bs were in agriculture and business management; the As were in core science, mathematics, geography, economics, and financial accounting; and the C was in English. English was my best and worst grade.

I was a reserved boy, but my excitement was impossible to conceal as I stared at my exam results. My eyes widened and my lips curled into a shy smile as I read the results one more time. My heart was racing as hope bloomed inside me - I could attend university in the Gambia or abroad.

I immediately visited our financial accounting teacher, Mr. John S. Kemokai, in his office to share the good news. He congratulated me and even informed me that the school principal was impressed with my results.

We walked to the principal's office, where he greeted me with a warm smile and a firm handshake. Standing before the principal, I felt a sense of pride. His congratulations were like music to my ears. He looked at me with admiration, and I knew I had impressed him with my performance.

But there was something else in his eyes that I couldn't quite place. It was as if he was not very familiar with my face. And that was not surprising, as I was a quiet boy from Commerce-One, not someone from Commerce-Two or the Science classes.

The principal went on to inform me that I had achieved the third-best results in the entire school; two boys were ahead of me, Abdul Nassir from the Science-One class who had 8 As and Saikou Touray from the Commerce-Two class with 6 As.

Excitedly, I took my results to Uncle Kemo and Malick, who were highly impressed with my achievements. I knew my parents would be just as thrilled and proud of my exam success. It was incredible to know that all my hard work, dedication, and focus had paid off.

I held onto the hope that my hard work would ultimately secure me a government scholarship to further my education at the University of The Gambia. I imagined attending the university, sitting in an economics class, and engaging in lively discussions with my professors.

The following year, I attended another graduation ceremony at Nusrat, thrilled to receive two awards. I was recognized as the third-best student in the school and for being the overall best in financial accounting. As I walked up to the stage to receive my awards, this time, I did so with a newfound confidence. It was another proud moment for my family and me.

Today, as I look back on my high school years, I feel a flood of emotions. The memories of my family, friends, and teachers are all so clear in my mind, and I realize now how much each of them played a crucial role in my journey. My parents were always there for me, offering their support in every way possible. They prayed for me to be blessed with kind and supportive people as I journeyed in life, and I am so grateful that their prayers have been answered since high school.

My supportive friends and teachers helped me overcome the challenges I faced and gave me the determination to succeed. It's all thanks to Kemo Ceesay, who believed in me and kickstarted my journey in high school by covering the full cost. I will always be grateful for their role in my educational journey.

However, one thing that stood out a few months later was that no one ever told me how hard life would be after high school.

CHAPTER THIRTEEN

LIFE AFTER HIGH SCHOOL IS HARD

IN TALLINDING. As I sat in my room, glancing at my high school textbooks and notes, I couldn't help but feel unsure about what lay ahead in my future. I had always been a top student at Nusrat High School, with a near-perfect transcript and a deep passion for accounting and economics. But now, as post-high school life loomed on the horizon, I faced a difficult question: what do I do next?

I knew I wanted to pursue higher education, but the options were limited. The free institutions in the Gambia, such as Gambia College and the School of Nursing, did not offer any courses in my desired field of Economics or Finance. And the tuition fees for the Management Development Institute and the University of the Gambia were astronomical.

Feeling lost and alone, I turned to my high school accounting teacher, Mr. John Kemokai, for guidance. He recognized my potential and offered me a position as a teaching assistant in business management and accounting at Nusrat High School.

The teaching allowance I received from the school helped me to start saving and even send some money to my parents in the village. A few months later, I decided to invest in a bicycle. This was a game changer for me, as it helped reduce my transportation expenses. I could now ride my bike to and from school. The teaching opportunity provided me with a sense of purpose and direction. It allowed me to grow under the guidance of an experienced mentor.

At that time, the University of the Gambia (UTG) had a flexible payment practice that allowed students to attend classes without paying the full tuition, but they held on to class transcripts or results until the tuition was paid. I found this fair and decided to apply to study economics and finance at UTG.

I continued teaching at Nusrat High School while attending classes at UTG. I chose UTG because it would be easier to acquire a scholarship from the government, considering my good grades in high school.

In the first semester, I scoured through the musty pages of newspapers in the UTG library for any mention of scholarships; my eyes darted back and forth, scanning. I listened intently to the national radio, eagerly awaiting announcements of new scholarship opportunities. I found and applied for countless scholarships, both announced by the national scholarship board and those posted on the UTG notice board. But, to my disappointment, none of my applications received a response. I began to wonder if someone was deliberately thwarting my efforts or if the scholarship committees were basing their decisions on factors other than performance.

If there had been a national ranking based on high school results, I would have ranked among the top 4 students in the country for the year I finished high school. I also knew the boys who had taken first and second place in Nusrat High School had traveled or begun a professional accounting course outside the university. Therefore, despite my strong academic record, I could not understand why my scholarship applications were unsuccessful.

At this point, I began to appreciate what arts students called nepotism, and its pervasive presence in society. If the country was genuinely committed to promoting education and combating poverty, special scholarships should be available at the University of the Gambia to support needy students.

This experience with government and government-related scholarships left me feeling disheartened and disillusioned. Despite having excellent results, I could not secure the scholarship I needed to pursue higher education in the country.

I realized that more than good results were needed to gain access to higher education, especially when it came to government-funded scholarships. The system was rigged against me, and other students like me who had worked hard and achieved academic success but could still not secure the support they needed to continue their studies.

This experience made me appreciate the importance of fighting for fair access to education and the need to address systemic biases that were preventing students of disadvantaged backgrounds from reaching their full potential.

Despite my setbacks and disappointment in securing government scholarships, I refused to give up. I wrote to private sector companies, banks, non-governmental organizations, and state-owned enterprises like Gamtel and Social Security, hoping that one of these institutions could offer me the support I needed to further my education. But, to my dismay, none of them came to my rescue.

I began to feel that the entire system was working against my desire to pursue higher education. I was aware that some state-run institutions sponsored their employees to study abroad, yet none of them deemed my high school achievements and results worthy of offering me a scholarship to study at UTG. I applied for jobs at some of these institutions, but I was not even offered a position as a cashier.

I met some scholarship recipients whose high school grades were not as good as mine and soon concluded that the difference between them and me was that their parents were financially better off. My parents were small-scale farmers from a rural village, while in contrast, their parents were often civil servants.

I felt lost and devastated. If depression had been as widely accepted and recognized in The Gambia as malaria, I would have been declared depressed. I had to decide whether to give up on my dream of higher education or find another way to keep going.

But I recovered and continued to hold fast to my belief that obtaining a higher education would bring about transformative changes for me and my community. I envisioned a brighter future for my children, filled with new opportunities and a different narrative.

I threw myself into my studies with renewed determination, balancing the multiple demands of university, part-time teaching, and my relentless search for a sponsor. The journey was not easy, but the unwavering support of my closest friends buoyed me. Abdou Qadri Ceesay, Ansuman Cham, and Habibatou Drammeh were my pillars of strength, sounding boards, and confidants. They supported me above and beyond to ensure I could continue at the university. This trio provided extra copies of lecture notes to aid my preparation for exams and revision. They were my support system; I couldn't have continued at the university without them.

As I look back on my immediate life after high school, I am filled with a deep sense of gratitude. It was a moment of pivot or perseverance. A moment when counselling became more important than any other agenda. Thanks to the kindness of friends and mentors, I persevered. They showed me that real friendship is limitless, and even in the darkest hours, hope shines eternally.

CHAPTER FOURTEEN

THE FIRST BANKER FROM MY VILLAGE

THE TIME WAS 8 P.M. ON SATURDAY. As I walked down the streets, the cool night air brushed against my skin and the moon shone brightly overhead, casting a pale glow over everything in its path. I was returning to my house from visiting my uncle. I eagerly looked forward to another movie night at the small cinema outlet opposite our compound. It was the only form of entertainment I felt at ease with, and my mind was wholly preoccupied with the thought of it.

But as I opened the compound gate, I felt that something was amiss. And as I got closer, my suspicions were confirmed: my front door was hanging open, broken, and splintered. I felt a cold sweat break out on my forehead.

I hesitated momentarily, trying to replay the evening's events and determine if I had forgotten to lock the door before leaving for my uncle's house. But deep down, I knew that I had closed the door. Someone had deliberately broken into my home.

I pushed open the door and stepped inside. The flickering light of a candle cast long shadows on the walls and floor. I could see that the place had been ransacked, with my bed sheet on the floor and my books scattered on the table. My bicycle, which I had parked just inside the door, was gone, as was my gas bottle.

I felt a wave of anger and betrayal as I surveyed the damage. The sense of loss and violation was overwhelming. I felt dejected, devastated, and defeated. As I sat there, the sound of the night seemed to press in on me from all sides, dull and distant. My mind was a jumbled mess, and I had no idea what I wanted to do next. All I knew was that the pain and sorrow I felt were like a heavy burden on my chest, and I wanted to scream it out, to let it all out in one anguished cry.

But I knew that I couldn't do that. I was a man, and as a man, I was expected to be strong and to keep my emotions in check. If I let out a cry of pain, I would be seen as weak, and I couldn't bear the thought. So, I sat there in silence, my mind and my heart in turmoil, struggling to understand what had happened.

That bicycle was vital to my earning a living. The bike took me to school to teach and took me to the nearby university lectures in Kanifing. My only tool for a smooth journey through my education had been hijacked, leaving me stranded in a turbulent and difficult struggle. I hated and cursed that thief.

With a sense of finality, I knew that my life at the university had come to an end. I felt like a door had closed, and my dreams and aspirations had been snatched away. I couldn't help but imagine how my life would play out.

I thought of relocating to Brikama College to study for the Higher Teachers Certificate (HTC) and become a teacher. I also considered going to the village and becoming a clerk on the Sapu agricultural campus next to my village. None of these options seemed to fit, and I couldn't shake off the feeling that I was meant to study economics and finance.

The theft of my bicycle significantly impacted my life. I had to reduce the number of courses I took at the university, making it more challenging for me to keep up with my studies. I continued working as a part-time teacher at Nusrat High School, which was only an hour's walk from my house.

AT THE RIGHT PLACE. One sunny Saturday afternoon as I was teaching financial accounting to a group of grade 12 students and delving deeper into the complexities of balance sheets and income statements, I noticed a figure standing outside the window, peering in at me. My curiosity got the better of me, and I turned to get a better look at the person. To my surprise, I recognized him as none other than Omar Jassey, a senior banker, chartered accountant, lecturer at the esteemed Nusrat Management Accountancy Training Centre (NMATC), and an alumnus of Nusrat High School.

As soon as I made the connection, I felt nervous, as if I were presenting strategy in front of Professor Michael Porter, who is closely watching my every word and gesture. But I pushed through and continued to deliver my lesson with precision, determined not to make any mistakes. After a few minutes of observation, Omar eventually turned away from the window and left.

Once my class ended, I went to Mr. Kemokai's office, where I often took a break. As I walked in, I was surprised to find Omar sitting in the office, waiting for Mr. Kemokai. I greeted Omar with a quiet nod. Omar broke the silence with a question: "What is your name?" I responded quickly, "My name is Ebrima Sawaneh." He asked if I was a trained accounting teacher or an accounting technician. I replied no to both possibilities. He then told me he thought I was a brother to one of his friends, Alieu Jobe, as we looked alike. Alieu was also a chartered accountant at the Gambia Accountant General Department and a lecturer in accounting at NMATC.

I felt honored when Mr. Omar asked me about myself, expressing an interest in getting to know me better. I eagerly hoped that he would ask more questions. However, our conversation ended when Mr. Kemokai walked into the office. "Good afternoon, Omar. Good afternoon, Ebrima," he greeted us as he took his seat.

Kemokai formally introduced me to Omar, putting in a good word for me and praising my level of intelligence and hard work. He concluded by noting that I was struggling with my tertiary education because I lacked funding. He politely asked if Omar could let us know as soon as any cashier employment opportunities existed at the bank where he worked.

Mr. Kemokai is a very kind-hearted person. I respected him a lot, even before the introduction to Omar. He must have seen something in me; he believed people like me were meant to be helped and elevated. First, he offered me an assistant teacher role in Nusrat, and now he was supporting me in getting a job. I felt grateful.

As I sat listening to Omar speak, I felt a sense of hope blooming within me. He told me about the upcoming Guaranty Trust Bank Serrekunda branch opening and the need for cashiers. Omar suggested I bring my high school exam results to him at the bank's headquarters and said he would talk to the human resources manager. However, he also clarified that the bank preferred to recruit candidates who had completed at least the foundation stage of professional certifications like the AAT and CAT and that there was a mandatory entrance test.

As I left the office that day, I felt a sense of excitement and anticipation. Throughout that weekend, getting a job was number one on my prayer list. The following Monday, I went to the bank. When I walked into the GTBank headquarters, I felt like I was in a different world. The floors, the high ceilings, and the impeccable decor were unlike anything I had ever seen. As instructed, I handed Omar my results, transcripts, and a meticulously crafted one-page resume.

A few days later, my phone rang, and I received an invitation to visit the bank for an entrance examination. The exam was primarily focused on testing my proficiency in the English language and my understanding of business mathematics, such as ratios and compound interest. I sat for the examination and emerged victorious, having scored highly.

About a week after the test, while browsing at the bustling internet cafe on the university library with my friends, I received a call from Amie Jallow, the human resources manager of the bank. She extended an invitation to me for an interview. Aunty Amie, as we affectionately referred to her, had a powerful command of the English language. Her eloquent voice was easily recognizable even through the static of my trusty Nokia 3310 phone.

Though I was thrilled at the news of the interview, I also felt a twinge of fear, as I was worried that the bank work would require advanced accounting knowledge. Additionally, if they were to ask for a professional certification like AAT, which I did not possess, my chances of success would be slim. For these reasons, I kept the news to myself and decided not to share it with my friends or family. I didn't even want them to know that I had attended an interview since I didn't feel confident that I could secure the job.

The interview day arrived, and I was torn on what to wear. I had seen bankers dressed in elegant corporate suits, so I chose to wear my old, worn suit to my interview. The suit was made of a thick, tweed fabric as strong as an old raincoat. I put on the suit and looked in the mirror. I didn't look like a banker, but I looked like someone who was serious about getting a job. I took a deep breath and headed out the door.

I arrived at the interview early and waited in the lobby. I watched the other candidates arrive, all dressed in better suits.

As I engaged in conversations, I soon realized that most of the other candidates had a foundation certificate in accounting. I was the only one without qualifications besides a high school certificate. I felt a bit self-conscious, but my high school grades in accounting and math boosted my confidence.

In the interview room, Aunty Amie exuded a warm and welcoming aura, immediately putting me at ease. The other interviewers' friendly smiles also seemed to communicate, "*We're here to learn about you, not intimidate you.*" This comforting ambiance made me feel a genuine connection with them, knowing that I wasn't merely a name on a resume but a person with unique stories and aspirations.

As the conversation unfolded, I immersed myself in a dialogue that assessed my skills and qualifications and delved into thought-provoking on team player, leadership, and service delivery. Engaging in such stimulating discussions expanded my knowledge, leaving me with valuable insights and perspectives I hadn't considered before.

As I left the interview, I felt a sense of relief and satisfaction. I had been dreading this interview for days, but it turned out to be more manageable than anticipated. I also had the opportunity to meet new people.

A few days after the interview, I received a phone call from Aunty Amie asking me to pick up my offer letter from the bank. I was filled with such excitement and joy that I could barely sleep that night.

The following day, I made my way to the GTB head office. Aunty Amie handed me an appointment letter. To my surprise, my name and address were meticulously printed on the letter, dated August 26, 2004, and signed by the Human Resources Manager and Assistant General Manager. The offer was for an annual salary that was a staggering increase of over 500% from my previous teaching allowance!

Aunty Amie kindly reminded me to take the letter home and that I had seven days to accept the offer and confirm my start date. Although I had learned the basics of contract law in high school, I couldn't afford to wait even a moment longer. I accepted the offer immediately. At the time, I wasn't concerned about the other employment terms and conditions or the possibility of salary negotiation. The bank management was doing me a great favor despite my lack of qualifications. The financial offer was too good to pass up.

As I was saying goodbye to Aunty Amie and leaving her office, she asked me a crucial question. "Do you have enough suits?" I replied that I only had one suit, the same one I had worn to the interview. She kindly advised me that I needed more than one and some long sleeves. Then she pulled out her handbag from her desk drawer and handed me some crispy new banknotes. It was 2,000 dalasi. "Take this as a loan and buy yourself some new clothes," she said. I was overwhelmed with gratitude, but it was more than that. I felt like she saw something special in me.

I quickly went to Mr. Kemokai's office in Nusrat to share the exciting news with him. He was thrilled and even called Omar to share in the celebration. With excitement, I hastened to share the news with my friends, Uncle Kemo, and Malick. Their elated reactions only added to my already high spirits.

I called my mother through one of the village's fixed telephones the next day. "Mummy, I have got a job in a big bank," I announced. She was excited. I could hear her smile over the phone. She must be smiling with hope. The hope that very soon the family's financial situation will improve. The hope that the other children will not struggle with school fees as I did. After taking a deep breath, she gave me her usual encouragement and support—her prayers. She prayed that the new job would be the start of a long string of successes in my life and that I would amass wealth to benefit those around me. My mother also reminded me of my humble roots. She cautioned me to perform my job duties to the best of my abilities and to be mindful of other people's hard-earned money. Like most villagers, my parents always taught us to be content with what we had. Despite knowing my character, my mother warned me to be cautious. As the saying goes in Gambia, "No matter how fast a horse rides, the rider still pressures the horse to ride faster."

The following weekend, I met with Omar at Nusrat, who advised me on preparing for my new role at the bank. He informed me of the necessary purchases I would need to make, such as formal attire. Omar kindly invited me to his home where he presented me with a suit, a pair of shoes, and several ties. The suit was much higher quality than I had worn for my interview and was a perfect fit, as Omar and I had similar body and shoe sizes. In addition to the clothing, Omar strongly advised me to start studying for an accounting technician course as soon as possible.

FIRST DAY AS A BANKER. I rose before the sun on that fateful morning, eager to face the challenges ahead. I indulged in a revitalizing shower and donned my crisply ironed long-sleeved shirt, ready to make a good impression. Yet, as I reached for my necktie, I soon discovered that the art of knot-tying was totally different from tying a stick of firewood in the village. My fingers fumbled as I struggled to replicate the knot. Despite my persistent efforts, I could only produce a knot that seemed to be barely holding on.

Just as I was about to head out the door, I was stopped by my friend and housemate, Alieu Bayo. He looked at my knot and declared that it was poorly done and that I appeared to have a rope around my neck. The two of us attempted to correct the situation, but to no avail. I eventually decided to redo the knot to the best of my ability and headed out, filled with a newfound confidence in my appearance.

As I arrived at the bank promptly on time, I was greeted by the HR team and introduced to my new supervisor, Mafuji Jammeh. To my relief, Mafuji immediately took notice of my necktie and expertly retied it, ensuring it was done correctly. He then introduced me to the Transaction Services Unit (TSU) team. It was a privilege to meet Mariama T. Jobe, who became my trainer. She guided me through the intricacies of the GTBank systems and procedures, making me feel at ease and confident in my new role.

THE FIRST BANKER FROM MY VILLAGE

When I got the credit of the first salary into my bank account, it felt grateful like a child who receives a present on their birthday. I immediately thought of my parents, and, with a humble heart, I sent a portion of the salary to them.

I then withdrew 2,000 dalasis to repay Aunty Amie. I knew her loan had helped me when I was starting, and I wanted to show my appreciation. But when I went to her office, she brushed off my gesture and asked me to take the money.

"It was not a loan," she said. "It was a gift from me to help you get started."

I was surprised. I had always thought that Aunty Amie had lent me the money, but now she told me it was a gift. I didn't know what to say.

"I don't know how to repay you," I said.

"You don't have to repay me," she said. "Just keep working hard and making your parents proud."

I smiled. "I will," I said.

She also revealed that management had taken a chance on me, offering me the job even though I lacked the minimum qualifications. She said they were impressed by my high-school achievements, bank entrance examination scores, and interview performance. With a motherly tone, Aunty Amie encouraged me to work hard, persevere, and continue learning by enrolling into one of the accounting courses.

I was speechless and overwhelmed by her and the bank management's outpouring of kindness. My thoughts raced to Kemokai, Omar, and now Aunty Amie, who had shown me such generosity. The only words I could muster were simple yet heartfelt: "Thank you once again." My face must have been a picture of surprise, reflecting the depth of my gratitude.

UNIVERSITY CLASSES. I found it difficult to balance my work and university commitments. As a banker, I often worked long hours that extended into the evening. This made it challenging to attend any class in the university. Unfortunately, the university did not offer part-time courses, so I had to withdraw from my studies there. Despite this setback, my desire to further my education beyond my high school certificate remained steadfast, especially with Omar and Aunty Amie encouraging me.

Determined to pursue my goal, I evaluated my options for continuing my education in accounting. I considered studying AAT, CAT, and ACCA, as these programs were highly sought after by those looking to secure a job in banking. I decided to enter the CAT program and traveled to the GAMTEL internet cafe in Serrakunda to complete my online registration. I purchased a bank draft and took it to the Nusrat Management Accountancy Training Centre (NMATC) with a copy of my documents. By January 2004, I was officially enrolled in the CAT program and eagerly working towards my new educational goals.

As I reflected on the rapid pace of change in my life and my newfound plans, I couldn't help but think of my father's words of wisdom regarding kindness to others. He believed that one didn't need to know someone to extend kindness to them and that the kindness shown by parents can have a lasting impact on their children elsewhere. I remembered many instances when my father would ask us to give up our rooms for visitors, even if he did not know them, as a demonstration of hospitality. He often explained this as part of Islamic tradition and counseled us that when we traveled, we too may encounter a kind soul who does not know us. I saw his words and prayers manifest in my life through the kindness of people like Kemokai, Omar, and Aunty Amie. This job offer marked the beginning of my journey towards realizing my dreams.

PART THREE

You don't become a master because you're able to retain knowledge. You become a master when you're able to release it.
— Steven Bartlett

CHAPTER FIFTEEN

BALANCING WORK AND STUDY

As the year turned over to a fresh start, I felt a surge of resolve. I rekindled my determination to excel in my educational and work pursuits and was determined to make the most of the new year. Despite the challenges ahead, I was eager to embark on my journey of combining a full-time banking job with pursuing higher education.

I found myself surrounded by like-minded individuals, all pursuing the common goal of furthering their education in accounting and finance. Some of my colleagues at the bank were already qualified accountants or were working towards their ACCA final level. This allowed me to expand my network and connect with these knowledgeable individuals. I was eager to learn from their experiences, be inspired by their achievements, and gain insight into their working systems. The collective wisdom and support of the learning community proved invaluable in my journey towards achieving my professional goals.

A few months into my role as a cashier, our supervisor, Mafuji Jammeh, resigned and relocated to the UK. This change brought a new face to the head office, as Mrs Kumba Secka Kebbeh was transferred from the Banjul branch to take on the role left by Mafuji.

Kumba was a formidable figure known for her unwavering discipline and strong leadership. Yet, despite her no-nonsense demeanor, she was also known for her kindness and compassion, earning her the respect and admiration of her colleagues. I was eager to continue growing under her guidance in my role and contributing to the team's success.

Each day, after meticulously balancing my cash box, I often offered to lend a hand to my fellow cashiers, particularly those struggling to reconcile their physical cash counts with the system. My attention to detail and background in accounting made me exceptionally skilled in detecting errors, and I was happy to help. My commitment to teamwork did not go unnoticed, and it came to the attention of Kumba, our supervisor.

One day, she called the entire unit together. She praised my dedication to the team and presented me with a cash appreciation gift as a token of her gratitude. This recognition further fueled my drive to excel. A few months later, I was given the opportunity to take on a new role within the bank: I was tasked with training new cashiers and reviewing their work, essentially serving as a deputy head cashier, though the title was not official.

This new position represented a crucial step in my learning and professional growth, as it brought me into contact with senior employees in the bank.

As I made connections and formed relationships within the bank, I had the privilege of meeting Mohamed Gillen, a highly regarded and well-respected senior employee. With his status as a chartered accountant and an executive member of the Gambia Association of Accountants (GAA), Gillen inspired many young people in the bank. I was lucky to have him as a mentor and friend.

Gillen was a true advocate for the education and professional development of those around him. He was always eager to share his vast banking, finance, and accounting knowledge. He would often call us to pose questions and deliver impromptu lectures to challenge our understanding of our work. These interactions were always enlightening and educational, as Gillen provided us with insightful advice and guidance.

He encouraged us to take our studies seriously and saw the value in pursuing a professional accounting program. His unwavering support inspired many of us to strive for excellence. I speak for many when I say that Gillen profoundly impacted our lives and careers.

Pursuing a professional qualification came at a high cost. The annual membership dues, examination fees, textbooks, and tuition fees all added up to a substantial sum.

As a self-sponsored student, managing this cost constantly challenged me. However, I was determined to succeed and found ways to make it work.

Sometimes, I deferred my exams until I had saved enough money. At other times, I would attend classes during one session and defer the exam to the next session. Eventually, I switched to self-study after completing level two of the ACCA. This allowed me to save on tuition fees while gaining the knowledge I needed to succeed. My friends and ex-trainees, Malick Ceesay and Saikou Manneh would sometimes assist in getting the ACCA books from the UK. I would reimburse them by the end of the month.

On one occasion, my exam payments were nearly late. As I made my way to Gillen's office with a folder in hand, I felt a sense of nervousness. After all, I needed him to sign the bank draft for my exam fees, and it was perilously close to the ACCA deadline for such payments.

Upon reading the supporting documents, he quickly realized I had requested the draft. He turned to me with a questioning look as he noticed the imminent ACCA deadline for such payments.

"Why are you paying your fees so late?" he asked, his pen hovering above the signature line. I explained to him that I had been waiting for my salary to hit my bank account before proceeding with the payment. I attempted to assure him that everything would be promptly taken care of.

Gillen's face softened into a friendly smile as he listened to my explanation, and I knew he had more to say on the matter.

"Next time you find yourself in this situation, come see me," he said, offering support. "I can help you with the ACCA payment, and you can settle with me at your convenience." He returned the folder to me, and I left his office with a newfound sense of comfort and gratitude.

Gillen's offer was a lifesaver, allowing me to save and repay him later. And true to his word, he supported me each time I needed help with my ACCA payment. I repaid him as we had agreed as soon as my salary arrived at the end of each month. But on the third occasion, to my surprise, he asked me to keep the money. I was left speechless and overwhelmed by this unexpected gesture. The amount, a hundred pounds, was no small sum, and I couldn't understand why Gillen would so generously give it to me. My mind raced with thoughts as I stood before him, trying to grasp the magnitude of his kindness.

Curious about the reason behind Gillen's charitable behavior, I eventually mustered the courage to ask him. His response was simple yet profound. "Don't follow the money. Always follow people," he said with a wise twinkle in his eye. "The best relationships give everything. Having money without anyone by your side is like having nothing at all."

His words struck a chord. His wisdom reminded me of the importance of forming meaningful connections with others and the fulfillment that comes from helping those in need.

Gillen's words echoed the same sentiments that my mother had instilled in me from a young age. She always reminded me, "A poor man with a relationship is better than a wealthy man with no relationship." Her teachings emphasized valuing relationships and maintaining close bonds with loved ones.

In GTBank, I was fortunate to have the opportunity to learn from many individuals, including our divisional head, Mr. Bolaji Ayodele. Under his leadership, monthly operations group training was introduced, with a test every six months. I thrived in this environment and consistently placed first in all three tests I participated in. This recognition as an emerging talent within the bank led to fast-paced growth opportunities, as I was given a chance to experience all areas of banking operations. Over the course of three years, I was promoted three times.

MY FRIENDS. Dr. Kebba S. Camara, a childhood friend of mine, became one of the longest friendships I have had outside my village. I first met Kebba in eighth grade at Brikamaba Junior School, where he was a brilliant student who sometimes ranked first in our class. Kebba, a young boy with a highly competitive spirit, was always eager to befriend anyone with a good book he did not have. Our friendship deepened when I let him borrow my brother's school notes, which he wanted to read ahead of the class.

After junior school, Kebba enrolled at Gambia High School while I attended Nusrat High School. Despite going to different schools, we lived in the same neighborhood of Tallinding, which allowed us to stay connected. Our friendship grew stronger when we started studying together in grade eleven. I enjoyed spending my evenings with Kebba's host, the Sawo family, the nicest people I could have asked to be around.

Even after Kebba traveled to the USA to pursue his education, I continued to visit his family, especially on weekends.

In the Sawo family, I met a young girl who was learning to cook. Her cooked rice sometimes led to complaints and boycotts by some people. Yet I was one of the few people who would eat her cooked food with praise. Over time, she became one of the best cooks in the family. She also became a strong and confident Muslim girl who wore a veil covering her head and shoulders, revealing only her face. Her name is Ndey Amie Sawo.

Amie and I sometimes see each other in their house, but we didn't really become close until her cousin sister, Fatoumata Touray, moved into Amie's compound. Fatoumata was from the same village as Kebba, but we were also junior school classmates in Brikamaba. She relocated to Amie's compound during my second year of working at GTB.

In one scorching summer, fate dealt me a hand that would change my life forever. Amie was struck by malaria and was admitted to the hospital. Compelled by a deep-rooted concern for her well-being, I visited her at the hospital, bearing gifts of fruit and kindness. Thereafter, we became friends.

Amie and I found ourselves inexorably drawn together as we grew more familiar. There was something about Amie that I was drawn to. She was kind, funny, and religious. I knew I was falling in love with Amie, but I was hesitant to tell her. I didn't want to ruin our friendship or her family's respect for me. But one day, I couldn't hold it in any longer. I told her how I felt, and she said she felt the same way. We were inseparable after that.

As I continued my ACCA studies in The Gambia, I noticed that many of my peers and colleagues in the bank had taken the opportunity to further their education by traveling abroad. This was partly due to the country's lack of educational institutions that offer a full ACCA course, particularly in advanced subjects. This realization prompted me to set my sights on traveling abroad to complete my ACCA course, even if I had to do so with limited financial standing.

After a tireless search for colleges and scholarships, I was overjoyed to receive an acceptance letter from a college in Canada with a partial scholarship. With eager anticipation, I journeyed to Dakar, brimming with hope for the future. I invested weeks of my time and resources preparing to make the trip, but my dreams were suddenly dashed when my visa application was rejected due to insufficient funding and no ties to my home country.

The rejection was a crushing blow, filling me with disappointment and sadness. But in that moment of disappointment, I found the strength to rise above my circumstances. I redoubled my commitment to education and determined to complete my ACCA program in the Gambia.

With unwavering dedication, I threw myself into self-study. I borrowed money from GTBank to fund my level two papers. Group studies with my coursemates proved valuable, but I also used my early mornings at the office for reading and studying.

My relentless efforts bore fruit when I completed ACCA Level 2, all while working at GTBank. This achievement was not only a source of pride but also led to a well-deserved promotion to the Executive Trainee level. Soon after, two more important events happened in my life. First, I mustered up the courage to pop the question, extending a marriage proposal to my beloved. Second, I received a job offer from Ecobank, a new banking institution. These momentous occasions marked a new chapter in my life, filled with love and professional growth.

CHAPTER SIXTEEN

THE ROAD TO START MARRIAGE.

Six short months after we started our relationship, Amie and I decided to plunge in and get married. It was a decision we made with our hearts, not our heads. We knew that we were young, but we also knew that we were meant to be together.

Amie was in her final year of high school, which made it unlikely for any parent to approve of the union. We were acutely aware that our decision to marry would cause some concern for her family. Despite the many compelling reasons why we should not wed, we followed the beat of our hearts and became impervious to reason.

We were met with mixed reactions as we broke the news of our impending marriage to both families. The Sawaneh family held the notion that Ebrima should not marry a girl from the city, especially one from a family they did not know. My parents were staunch supporters of the notion.

On the other hand, the Sawo family believed that Amie should not get married yet and should instead focus on her education. Her parents were the vocal supporters of this notion, while Amie stood firm in her resolve to marry the man she loved.

Determined to fight for our love, I switched tactics and opted for a more diplomatic approach. Malick and I reached out to our uncles, Uncle Mungel, my father's younger brother, and the late Uncle Kemo Keita, my dad's best friend, a strong Islamic scholar, and an Imam.

Uncle Kemo, who was based in the city, expressed his desire to visit Amie's parents before approaching my parents. He was keen on discussing the matter with them first, believing that they held the key to unlocking a resolution to our dilemma.

One evening, as the sun set, Amie's parents warmly welcomed Uncle Kemo into their home, as is customary for any esteemed elder. In a show of utmost respect, Amie fetched a cup of water. She presented it to Uncle Kemo, kneeling on both knees with her head fully covered. The act of Amie's was her true self, not packaging. The display of grace and humility left a lasting impression on Uncle Kemo.

As he introduced himself to Amie's father, Uncle Kemo tactfully avoided mentioning the sensitive debate in our family. He instead focused on getting to know the family and familiarizing himself with their way of life. It was a strategic move that he hoped would pay off in the end.

While we walked Uncle Kemo home that evening, he wasted no time announcing his decision. He assured us that he would send the cola nut, meaning a marriage proposal to Amie's family and that we would be married, even if my biological father opposed the union.

The very next day, Uncle Kemo made good on his word and called my father to inform him of his decision to get me married. My father gave us his blessings, and the marriage proposal proceeded.

Uncle Kemo's actions reminded me that blood ties do not solely define family relationships. It is the bonds of trust and respect that truly define and strengthen a relationship. I can only imagine the words exchanged between Uncle Kemo and my father. Still, his unwavering support and determination to see my father accept my choice of love demonstrated his strong relationship with my dad.

After a week of family discussions, Uncle Mungel sent a formal proposal to Amie's family. To our delight, the proposal was accepted. We were given a date and a comprehensive list of traditional requirements.

In the Gambia, it is customary for the groom to meet the bride's extended family before marriage. This meeting allows the groom to meet the bride's family for an introduction, get to know them better, and seek their blessings. Sometimes, the groom is expected to give something valuable, such as firewood, fabric, or cash, often with cola nut during the visit. This shows respect for the bride's family.

My brothers and friends in the village fetched firewood and took it to Amie's parents' villages. Malick and I visited the families in the city.

The bride's elderly relatives may also advise the groom during these meetings. The elders may offer words of wisdom about marriage and family life. One of Amie's uncles told me, "Blood is thicker than water." This means that family ties are more important than anything else. Her grandfather said, "A real man never hits a woman, no matter how angry he is." This is a reminder that violence is never the answer.

I found these words of advice to be very valuable. They helped me understand the importance of family and the need to treat my wife respectfully. I am grateful to the Sawo family for welcoming me into their home and sharing their wisdom.

On September 2, 2007, the two families finally exchanged vows in a traditional Islamic ceremony, with Uncle Kemo leading the way in Bundung mosque. Being practical and considerate, Amie and I decided to defer the wedding reception until she finished high school, giving me ample time to save for the event.

About a year later, we invited our dearest to the Tallinding Bantaba Nursery School to witness our love and commitment. It was a day of immense joy and happiness, a testament to the unwavering support of our families. The music was soft and beautiful, and the food was delicious. We were surrounded by people who loved us and felt truly blessed.

Reflecting on the journey to my marriage, I realize none of our parents were wrong in their concerns and expectations.

From the perspective of Amie's family, they wanted to ensure that their daughter received a good education. They were concerned about Amie's ability to get an education beyond high school. At that time, very few families in The Gambia could guarantee their daughters the opportunity to pursue higher education, especially if they got married during their final year of high school. Nonetheless, I am glad that Amie and I worked together to ensure she went on to complete her degree at Coventry University, UK. This achievement was attained through our partnership and continuous support.

On the other hand, my family was concerned about Amie's role in cementing our family relationships. They had heard stories about wives who did not allow their husbands to help their village families. They had also heard stories about sons who never visited their families in the village after they married in the city. These stories worried my family, and hence their hesitation about my choice.

The journey to start a family has made me realize that nothing is more powerful than combining prayer, diligent effort, and nurturing meaningful connections with others.

CHAPTER SEVENTEEN

NEW JOB & NEW LEVEL

As a young ambitious student of accounting and finance, I held a steadfast aspiration to work in the finance department of GTBank. Yet despite my eagerness to expand my horizons and take on new challenges, the management was determined to keep me within the Operations department, believing me to be one of the future leaders of the department. At that time, Faburama Ceesay, the Financial Controller of GTB, had attempted to transfer me to the finance department, but his efforts were unsuccessful. Rather than feeling discouraged by this restriction, I built a network with some finance team members to appreciate core finance and accounting activities.

Nonetheless, my time at GTBank proved to be a rich and rewarding experience, as I was given the opportunity to delve into various functions, such as international funds transfer, treasury operations, and accounting operations. Eventually, I was entrusted with the leadership of the trade finance operations unit, which allowed me to hone my skills to become a formidable force in the banking industry.

However, my passion for the finance function grew as I delved deeper into it through the ACCA studies. I knew I could not rest until I had explored every avenue available.

OPPORTUNITY. The Gambian banking industry was shaken up in October 2007 with the entry of a new player in the market, Ecobank Gambia Ltd. This bank generated a lot of buzz due to its pan-African banking model and extensive geographical presence across the continent. Ecobank's entry into the market proved to be a game-changer as it started recruiting talented employees from other established banks, including GTBank.

My mentors and friends, such as Mohammed Gillen, Alieu Awe, and Kumba Kebbeh, moved to Ecobank. Kumba reached out to me and extended an invitation to join her operations team. Meanwhile, Alieu Awe, the head of finance at Ecobank, wanted me to support him in setting up a new department. I was thrilled yet perplexed, being torn between these two options.

In the end, Mohammed Gilen and Arona John provided the clarity I needed to decide. Both recommended I join the bank, as Ecobank offered many learning opportunities and exposure I needed in my career.

Intrigued by Ecobank's opportunity, I agreed to an interview with the CEO, Fitzgerald Odonkor, a Ghanaian national. Fitz was a highly regarded expert in trade finance, having made his mark at Ecobank Ghana and across the group. During our meeting, we dug deep into trade finance. It quickly became evident that my skills and experience aligned with his expertise.

Fitz was impressed with my trade finance knowledge and recommended that I join the trade operations department, which reported directly to Kumba. He assured me that I would have the opportunity to switch to finance after training someone to take over my role in trade operations. This was a significant offer, as expert knowledge of trade operations, especially in areas such as letters of credit, was highly sought after in the Gambia.

I spent several days consulting with my wife and friends in both banks, weighing the pros and cons of each option. Ultimately, in December 2007, I decided to take the leap and join Ecobank. The prospect of leaving GTBank was challenging, as they offered me a promotion to assistant manager, indicating my value to their team. However, I also saw a unique opportunity to work in the core finance function of Ecobank, which could provide me with a new avenue for personal growth and learning.

My decision was about the next phase of my personal development and learning journey. Working in the finance department of a bank would allow me to apply the accounting knowledge I had gained from my ACCA studies.

Just two months after joining the Ecobank, my career unexpectedly changed. Alieu Awe, the Head of Finance, called me into his office and proposed a unique opportunity. He negotiated with the operations department to loan me to the finance team until trade operations volumes increased. It was a dream come true. I became the second employee of Ecobank Gambia's finance department. Although Alieu never paid back the "borrowed" headcount from operations, his decision aligned me with my career path.

As I settled into my new role, I was tasked with setting up all the local processes, procedures, and reporting for the finance team. The learning curve was steep as I became familiar with Ecobank Group policies and software. In addition, I was studying for the ACCA Level 3 certification, which added another layer of complexity to my already challenging role.

A few months later, Alieu nominated me to attend training in Ghana. This experience was momentous, marking the first time I would ever step foot on an airplane.

The morning of our departure was early; we arrived at the airport with ample time before the flight, as stated on our tickets. I checked in at the counter and then passed through immigration, where my international passport received its first airport stamp.

Upon receiving my boarding pass, I was surprised to find that I had been assigned a particular seat number. I would have eagerly rushed to secure a spot if we had been traveling by van instead of an airplane.

We finally boarded the airplane an hour later, and I took my designated seat. I found fastening my seatbelt quite challenging, but luckily, my colleague Sanna Touray came to my rescue. After the necessary protocols were completed, the

NEW JOB & NEW LEVEL

airplane finally took off. I gazed out the window to take in the breathtaking view of the tiny city houses and cars below us.

As I gazed out of the airplane window, my mind drifted back to my childhood days in the village. I remembered how we used to spot planes high up in the sky, those specks amidst the vast blue expanse. We'd point excitedly and shout to our friends, eager to share the thrill of seeing an airplane soaring above us. My imagination never ventured beyond that momentary glimpse of a distant plane back then. I couldn't fathom what it would be like to sit inside one. Education and hard work eventually led me to a job that allowed me to experience flying in a plane myself.

As I looked out at the clouds and the earth far below, I wondered if there were other young kids doing the same thing today - pointing at planes in the sky, shouting with excitement, their imaginations set free. It was a beautiful reminder of how dreams can take flight, like those planes in the sky, carrying us to places we once could only dream of.

However, my excitement soon gave way to fear mid-flight when we hit turbulence. The plane shook as if we were on a road with potholes, and we were instructed to fasten our seatbelts. As I clung to the arms of my seat, I imagined the worst-case scenario: a catastrophic crash to the ground.

In those tense moments, I recited every prayer I knew, silently hoping for a safe landing. Eventually, the turbulence subsided, and the captain signaled that we could remove our seatbelts. Although I felt a sense of relief, I was still too scared to unfasten mine until we finally touched down at the Kotoka International Airport in Accra.

Our trip to Ghana was an incredible experience with immersed in learning and networking for one week with a community of fellow Ecobankers from different countries. As the week ended, we returned home.

As Ecobank's activities continued to grow, my responsibilities in the office increased, leaving me with little time for anything else. Even enrolling in evening classes for the ACCA was impossible, as I often worked late into the night. However, I was determined to complete the program, so I decided to continue through self-study.

This busy period coincided with Amie and I moving in together after she completed high school. As a self-study student, I had to dedicate more time to my studies than most other students. After arriving home from work around 8 p.m., I would sit at the table and study until around 1 a.m. Amie would often be asleep by the time I finished my night studies. Although Amie was also enrolled in a human resources management course, our schedules were so busy that we barely had time for ourselves. But her understanding and support during this critical time were invaluable to me.

I invested heavily in ACCA Level 3, buying books from approved publishers in the UK and carefully selecting course papers to study. As someone who was quite skilled in mathematics, I combined a few calculation courses together. Additionally, I took a distance learning course with Kaplan International on UK advanced taxation. I also joined group studies and had ACCA members like Arona John and Alpha Jallow, who had the opportunity to study ACCA in London and were kind enough to share their old notes with me.

SURPRISE. I walked into our living room, and Amie was sitting watching television. She had a radiant smile. "Mansa," she said, her voice shaky with excitement. "I have something to show you."

My heart fluttered with anticipation. I sat down next to her, and she handed me an envelope. I carefully opened it and looked inside. It was a medical report, but I couldn't understand it.

"You are going to be a father," Amie said.

I looked at her, and my breath caught in my throat. I couldn't believe it. We were going to have a baby! I gazed into her eyes, and at that moment, our love unfurled like a blossoming flower. We were so happy, and we knew that our lives were about to change forever. We held each other tightly, and I felt tears welling in her eyes. This was the best day of my life.

Months later in 2009, while I was on another official trip to Nigeria, Amie and I welcomed our first baby, a girl. We named her Kumba, after Kumba S Kebbeh, my friend and manager.

According to Gambian tradition, a baby girl brings luck to the father. The following month, I received the exam results of my last two ACCA papers, which I passed. The result made me one of the very few students who had completed the ACCA program without having to retake a single exam. It was a happy moment both at home and in the office.

With the arrival of a new baby and a new qualification, my professional life took an upswing. I got promotions and pay raises. Job offers from other local banks came my way, but I declined them all.

CHAPTER EIGHTEEN

INTERNATIONAL JOB OPPORTUNITY

Employees often focus on acquiring qualifications, but employers truly value improved performance. After completing my ACCA qualification, I set out to master one core skill to supercharge my effectiveness at work. Microsoft Excel skill was like gold in the banking industry, but only a few understood Excel's potential beyond basic arithmetic. So, I decided that Microsoft Excel was going to be my area of expertise.

Determined to pursue this new learning goal, I purchased several Excel books on Amazon. I spent countless hours poring over these books, teaching myself advanced techniques, including creating VBA code to automate reports. I often lost myself trying to crack a particularly stubborn solution, and most times, this ate into my time with Amie and the baby.

My newfound proficiency in Excel, combined with my banking and finance knowledge, made me incredibly productive. I was able to complete reports and assignments with ease and efficiency through automation. Word of my Excel prowess quickly spread, and colleagues from other departments frequently sought my assistance. I even began offering Excel training sessions within Ecobank Gambia and sharing notes with colleagues in the Ecobank group.

My knowledge sharing efforts propelled my recognition within the bank and at the group office. I started to represent Gambia on software implementation projects. In July 2009, our new CEO, Esijolone Okorodudu, recommended I visit Nigeria to understudy their monthly management reporting pack. I completed the trip and successfully implemented a similar reporting system in The Gambia. Ecobank Group Finance Director Laurence do Rego visited The Gambia the following year. Thanks to Jolone and Alieu, I had the opportunity to present some of my work to her. Madam Rego was impressed with the report and even emailed me on her way to the airport about potential future group finance transformation projects I could participate in. Ecobank Sierra Leone later invited me to Freetown to train their staff in Microsoft Excel Application in Banking.

In addition to my day job, I started to teach the ACCA technician papers at the Nusrat Management Training Centre. Furthermore, with Alkali Bah and Bambo Samateh, we developed and lectured in the first banking and finance program at the Management Development Institute (MDI). These part-time teaching roles provided extra income and allowed me to continue self-improvement while supporting young people. Even after completing my ACCA course and assuming larger responsibilities within the bank, I continued to dedicate myself to teaching.

As I progressed in my career and my income increased, I found myself with more disposable income. While many of my peers were taking out loans to purchase cars, I decided to take a different approach. Owning a car was not a priority for Amie and me. Instead, I chose to invest in something that would significantly impact my family: I decided to take out a loan to build a house for my parents in the village. They needed a comfortable and secure place to call their own, and this was a more worthwhile investment. In addition, I used the remaining loan balance as a deposit for my first piece of land, which I acquired through the Social Security Housing Scheme in Tujereng.

Despite my level within the bank and the financial freedom that it brought, I chose not to purchase a car. Some of my colleagues occasionally suggested that I do so, but the satisfaction of providing a new home for my parents and investing in my future through property ownership far outweighed any need for a Tokunbo car. Additionally, I saw my buddy, Alpha Jallow, build a home before buying a car.

NEW MANAGER. Shortly after Alieu Awe left the bank to pursue an international job opportunity, the management team hired Mamat Jobe as his replacement. Mamat was working with Standard Chartered Bank Gambia (SCB) as the financial controller. I was already acquainted with Mamat, as he had once been my instructor during a CAT course on financial reporting. Little had I known then that our paths would professionally cross again.

Coincidentally, while Mamat was discussing with Ecobank, Standard Chartered Bank was also talking with me about a different job opportunity. Neither Mamat nor I knew about this situation until he joined the Ecobank team. As fate would have it, my offer from SCB arrived shortly after that, which presented me with a dilemma. While SCB offered better pay and benefits, including an official car, Ecobank held a special place in my heart due to the relationships I had built there.

As I deliberated over my decision, I sought advice from trusted people, including Mamat. I weighed the opinions of individuals who had worked in both institutions. Eventually, I decided to stay at Ecobank. And I'm glad I did, as this decision led to some of the most fulfilling experiences of my professional career.

Working alongside Mamat, we quickly developed a strong friendship and professional relationship. Together, we formed a dynamic team that produced some of the best work that Ecobank Gambia had ever seen. From the country level to the group office, our team produced one of the most efficient and cohesive departments within the Ecobank group. I am not surprised the finance department produces 4 times more expatriates than the other departments in Ecobank Gambia.

Mamat's influence on me extended beyond our professional achievements. Under his mentorship, I became more interested in reading materials on leadership and other soft skills while maintaining my Excel guru expertise. He invested

INTERNATIONAL JOB OPPORTUNITY

in our relationship, going out of his way to drive me home after work every day, even though our houses were in different parts of the city.

Despite the many benefits of working at Ecobank, as a young and ambitious accountant, I harbored a strong desire to grow my career beyond the confines of the small Gambian economy. Pursuing this goal, I applied for many opportunities within the Ecobank group and was even invited to interview for several roles. Despite my best efforts, however, I never secured another position within the group.

NAIJA. One Friday evening at around 9 p.m., I received an unexpected email from James Buchanan, offering me a job opportunity at a leading African sovereign financial institution based in Nigeria. I read through his message, which expressed confidence in my skills and qualifications. James explained that he had received my CV from a mutual contact, whom I never know the name of till today.

James believed I had all the right experiences to excel in this new institution, but he feared the role might be a little beneath me. He also assured me that, despite its novelty, the organization had great opportunities for young professionals like me.

Given the negative stereotypes portrayed about internet fraud and scams in Nigeria, I initially hesitated to believe there was a genuine job opportunity in Nigeria. However, two days later, I decided to respond to the email to express my interest. James quickly connected me to the institution, the Africa Finance Corporation (AFC), where I had several phone interviews with the team. Though I had doubts about the legitimacy of the process, I didn't think to conduct any research on AFC to verify its credibility through Google. I continued to play along with all seriousness because every time I spoke to them, I became convinced that they were genuine.

The following month, AFC invited me to a face-to-face interview with the AFC Director and Chief Financial Officer in Lagos. Although I had traveled to Nigeria twice before, I still felt that I was not a Lagos boy. Yet, the decision of AFC buying my air ticket provided some solace and ultimately led me to agree to make the journey.

The AFC HR team sent me the ticket a day before my flight. The ticket was pasted into the body of the email. Hence, I visited the airline's local office to verify if it was a genuine ticket. In the morning of the travel date, I loaded more recharge onto my mobile phone and activated roaming for the first time. With prayers for a successful trip during the holy month of Ramadan, I boarded my flight to Nigeria.

Upon arrival at the airport that night, I was relieved to find a friendly driver who had been sent to pick me up. He took me to a guesthouse in Ikoyi, where I spent the night. The following morning, we made our way to the AFC office. As we approached the building, I noticed the absence of a large signboard typically seen outside Nigerian banks on Victoria Island. Instead, the office building looked like a compound, with a barbed wire fence around it and several cars parked outside. This stirred a mix of emotions within me. But before I could fully process them, the driver entered the compound, and the security guard closed the gate behind us. I felt a chill run down my spine.

However, at the reception, I was warmly welcomed by Bisola, the HR Assistant, who ushered me into the office of Dr. Sola, the Chief Financial Officer. He offered me tea, which I politely declined, as I was fasting. Dr. Sola asked me a series of questions, all of which I answered to the best of my ability. At the end of the interview, he shared that other Gambians were already working at AFC, which piqued my interest. He then introduced me to two gentlemen, Batchi Baldeh and Amadou Wadda, who did not hesitate to show me Gambian style with a smile. This unexpected connection made me feel at ease and further fueled my interest in AFC.

In late August 2011, AFC made me a promising offer for an associate position. Despite having a good sense of the banking industry, I still felt I needed a fresh perspective on whether to accept the job. I sought the counsel of Amadou. His words depicted AFC's culture, growth opportunities, and rewards. After much thought, I ultimately decided to accept the job offer.

With my decision, it became time to inform Ecobank of my impending departure. Though I was thrilled to have landed an international job, I felt bittersweet about leaving behind a group of colleagues, with some of whom I had developed strong relationships. Additionally, Ecobank has sponsored me on numerous international and local training programs, which allowed me to build invaluable networks within the region.

Emotions ran high on the day of my send-forth meeting. Mareme Ndiaye, the CEO of the bank, praised my work and expressed her lack of surprise at my success, a gesture that meant a lot to me. As a gift to the team, I presented the CEO with a CD containing customized 100-page Microsoft Excel eBooks that I had written for Ecobank. It was a small token of my appreciation for the opportunity to have been able to work with such a wonderful group of people.

CHAPTER NINETEEN

THE ROAD TO NIGERIA

I was thrilled about my new job in Nigeria and excited for the adventure ahead. Nigeria has a strong story of rich cultural heritage, and the hardworking and entrepreneurial spirit that seemed to thrive among its people. What's more, with a population of over 160 million, the country presented an opportunity that would broaden my experience beyond the Gambia's modest population of two million.

But I wasn't just motivated by the allure of Nigeria's demographics, I was also impressed by the country's educational infrastructure, which I believed would provide my daughter with a better learning environment than what was available in the Gambia. Moreover, the job offer that took me to Nigeria represented a significant professional milestone I was eager to explore.

Before my family relocated, I had to find a suitable place that was foreigner and family friendly. I was the first person from outside Nigeria to join the AFC's finance and treasury division. The team was very welcoming and helpful, and they made sure that I settled in the country smoothly. My manager, Babajide Bola, gave up his weekends to help me search for an apartment. Babajide's attention to detail was not limited to the office. He rejected several apartments during our search. At some point, I was tempted to tell him, "*Oga, let us pick one, I am tired of staying in a hotel.*" However, we finally settled on an apartment in Lekki Phase 1. It was new, close to a supermarket, in a quiet location, and had good road access. More importantly, the landlord was very kind and accommodating. Babajide negotiated and reviewed the rental contract. Julius Owotuga recommended a lady who supported buying all the initial household items. The two gentlemen also ensured I got a vehicle that aligned with the company's policy. The CFO continuously seeks direct feedback on my settlement progress and office tasks.

There are two things in which the Gambia has a better supply than Nigeria: the original Gambian Jollof rice and the more stable electricity supply. In Nigeria, the first assets I bought were a generator and inverter because the electricity supply is not always reliable. I had never used a generator before, but I learned how to operate it in Nigeria. The experience also improved my technical skills, and now I have a toolbox for small plumbing and electrical work.

Furthermore, life in Nigeria without my family had its challenges, as I got food poisoning in the 2nd month. I suddenly felt excruciating pain on my way home from work. I tried to ignore it, but it felt as though something was piercing my intestines. I requested the driver to stop at a pharmacy on Awolowo Road in Ikoyi for medicine. Later, the driver left after dropping me home. But the pain persisted, preventing me from sitting upright. I reached out to Babajide, who promptly came to help and took me to Reddington Hospital. Thankfully, I had my medical insurance card, which enabled me to be admitted for a week. Despite my ordeal, I chose not to tell my family in the Gambia until after discharge. I feared the news would only worry them, especially my mom and Amie.

When Amie and Kumba finally joined me in Nigeria, I felt a moment of pure joy having my family with me and sharing the experience of living in this new environment together. With a settled home and some savings in my account, I decided to fulfill my father's lifelong dream.

As a devout Muslim, one of his greatest aspirations was to visit the holy city of Mecca, a wish many of his peers shared. With the help of my mother and brother Malick, we arranged for my father to embark on a pilgrimage to Mecca. To keep the surprise a secret, we told him that his travel to the city was required to obtain some documents for my new job. We needed him to acquire an international passport to make the journey to Mecca.

Once my father had secured his passport, Malick called for a family meeting in the village, where our uncle announced the news of my father's pilgrimage. Though I wasn't present, I imagined how my family felt upon hearing the news. I pictured uncles, aunties, brothers, and sisters gathering in the middle of the compound, eagerly awaiting the news. Prayers likely preceded the announcement, and I imagined the pride and joy that must have filled the air.

Months later, Amie and I decided to acquire another piece of land in Lamin Village. This was a significant milestone in our journey to financial independence, and we were fascinated by the prospect of building our first compound.

The compound was not just a physical structure but a symbol of our progress and financial freedom. It was a place to unite as a family, relax, and appreciate our growth. My parents were especially pleased with the new development, as they could now stay there whenever they traveled to the city.

Despite having a stable job and improved financial status, pursuing higher education remained my top priority. Additionally, the AFC's policy required a bachelor's degree as a basic requirement for all professionals, regardless of their qualifications. At that time, ACCA and Oxford Brookes University had a partnership that allowed ACCA students to write a research project and reflective statement to earn an accounting degree. Therefore, during the recruitment process, I had promised the AFC team that I would acquire a degree within six months. Although I first attempted the project in 2008, it was not successful. I focused on ACCA Level III at the time and never resubmitted the project. However, I reviewed and resubmitted the project in 2012 and was awarded a degree in applied accounting with second-class upper honors.

Beyond meeting the degree requirements set by the AFC, I recognized the importance of personal development in a competitive marketplace like Lagos. Observing that Nigeria had a more developed financial market than the Gambia, where I'd previously resided, I concluded that it was essential for me to sharpen my skills through higher education. Many of my colleagues had obtained their MBAs or were pursuing CFA programs. While CFA skills could be easily practiced in Nigeria, most knowledge would not apply to the Gambia market for a decade. Hence, I decided to pursue an MBA.

In order to obtain my MBA, I had to select the appropriate educational institution. My goal was to find a school that offered distance learning and fit within my budget, as I could not afford to leave my job to attend a full-time MBA program. With this heavy on my mind, I spent months searching the internet and ACCA journals for the perfect match. Then, I stumbled upon Edinburgh Business School (EBS), which seemed tailor-made for my needs.

EBS provided an excellent distance-learning program and offered special exemptions for ACCA members. Even more importantly, the program's cost was reasonable. It allowed payment per subject, a feature not commonly found in most MBA programs. Unlike other schools, EBS did not require students to write a thesis or short assignments for their MBA program. Instead, students took a three-hour exam on case studies and theories. I found this structure more manageable than the traditional method of thesis writing. I was confident that I had made the right choice by enrolling.

My first papers, Organizational Behavior and Economics, were followed by subsequent general and specialized courses.

The entire program was self-paced, but I did take advantage of some revision classes offered by a local EBS partner institution called EDC. These classes helped me reinforce my learning and provided networking opportunities with other MBA students in Nigeria.

I found the program highly educational and more challenging than anticipated. It shifted my mindset from that of a finance employee to that of a leader with an entrepreneurial mindset. This program inspired me to start a side hustle, as it is commonly known, but self-doubt held me back for some time.

Furthermore, as I pursued the MBA, AFC also provided me with numerous learning opportunities. I was sent for many short courses and seminars in Dubai, Europe, and the USA. AFC was like an MBA program, and I got the opportunity to meet many brilliant and experienced workers from across the globe, some of whom had worked for the world's most prominent financial institutions. Being in the company of such exceptional individuals was a learning opportunity like no other. The knowledge, experience, and perspectives they bring to the table inspire and challenge me.

I developed valuable relationships with mentors who helped guide me in my decision-making. I was fortunate to have senior Gambian colleagues at AFC, led by Oliver Andrews, who played a crucial coaching role in my career. Banji Fehintola was my official mentor through the AFC mentoring program, he continued to mentor me beyond the pilot phase. These relationships gave me the support and guidance I needed to find my way in the international corporate world. I realized how wise a decision I'd made when I chose to pursue a career in the AFC after leaving the Gambia. In 2015, I completed the MBA program with distinction, having specialized in finance.

CHAPTER TWENTY

PERSONAL DEVELOPMENT IS PERSONAL

Ayotunde Anjorin was the financial controller of AFC when I joined the corporation. Before AFC, Ayotunde worked at Standard Chartered Bank, where his role covered the subsidiary in the Gambia. I later discovered that had I accepted the job offer from Standard Chartered Gambia years earlier, Ayotunde would have been my regional line manager. However, fate had other plans. Ayotunde became my senior supervisor at AFC. We developed a close working relationship, especially after he was promoted to CFO.

One day, Ayotunde was invited to present at a prominent international bank. I helped him prepare his presentation slides, and after the event, the bank gave him a book called *Success Principles* by Jack Canfield. Ayotunde kindly gave me the book as a token of appreciation. I briefly glanced at the cover and placed it on my bookshelf, as my reading interests focused on finance, business, leadership, and related topics.

One evening, I finally decided to open the book. The first chapter, which focused on personal responsibility, caught my attention, and I read the entire book twice. I learned a lot from the book, especially about the fundamentals of personal success. I also realized I needed to work on other areas, like personal branding and public speaking.

Inspired by what I had read, I wanted to share my knowledge with others, especially young people in the Gambia, so I decided to start blogging. With the help of a colleague, Gregory, I purchased a domain for my first website, successvalues.com. Although Gregory was busy and could not give me his full attention, he shared resources that helped me learn about WordPress and basic website coding.

I learned how to operate my website and started writing about personal success, small business management, and personal finance. My site became the first personal development blog in the Gambia to target readers in the country. My blog even received press attention from a prominent local newspaper, and I was also invited to facilitate two sessions at the first Youth Entrepreneurship Summit in the Gambia.

Knowledge sharing is my core passion, and blogging was a great way to continue doing that, especially in the information age. When I was based in the Gambia, I mentored many of my students from MDI and Nusrat. Through my blog, I got the opportunity to share my experiences and new knowledge with even more people, both inside and outside the Gambia. Eventually, I registered a second blog called businessingambia.com. The objective was for successvalue.com to continue writing about personal development while the new blog will focus on personal finance and small business management topics.

One of the most popular articles on my first blog is titled "How to Pass a Professional Exam." This article was inspired by the many questions I'd received from students in the Gambia who were pursuing the ACCA program. I shared some strategies that worked for me, and the article was well received.

A few months later, I decided to turn the article into a book, but I needed to figure out how to go about publishing a book. I drafted and abandoned the first version of the book.

After conducting several online searches, I stumbled upon an online school called Self-Publishing School. I enrolled in their program, which taught me everything from the writing process to follow-up marketing strategies. With the new skills I acquired from the program, I published my book, *PASSED*, on Amazon in October 2017.

To my delight, by November of the same year, the book became an Amazon USA best-seller in three categories. I also partnered with Fulladu Publishers and Kachifo Limited to publish the book in the Gambia and Nigeria, respectively. It has since sold over 3,000 digital and print copies.

Writing and publishing the book allowed me to share knowledge, bring in additional income, and improve my brand. The book's success was once announced by Andrew Ali, the CEO of AFC at the time, during one of our town hall meetings. It received media coverage from major outlets in the Gambia, such as Fatu Network and, Gambia Radio and Television Services (GRTS), and Elite Media in Sweden. These are achievements that money cannot buy, and they have significantly impacted my life.

As I delved into personal development books, I came across various authors, such as Brian Tracy and Fela Durotoye, who greatly emphasized the significance of communication, particularly public speaking. These readings brought to mind an experience when I was at GTBank. I remember observing some employees struggling to present their ideas while visibly sweating under the cool air from the air conditioning system. It was apparent that they were afraid of speaking in public.

Among all my searches, joining an unconventional group called Toastmasters is the most effective and affordable method to enhance public speaking skills. Therefore, I joined the Seaside Toastmasters Club in Lagos to improve my leadership and public speaking skills. I was amazed by the Toastmasters feedback system and witnessed my skills improve through recording my speeches. I gained confidence as I learned to prepare and deliver stories. Within three years of joining the club, I progressed from being a member to becoming Vice President and then President of the Seaside Toastmasters Club. During my tenure as president, we faced one of the biggest challenges of our time, the COVID-19 pandemic. However, we successfully transitioned from physical to virtual meetings, ensuring the club's continued success.

As the COVID-19 pandemic continued to spread, Lagos, Nigeria's biggest city, implemented a total lockdown, and I had to start working from home. During this period, I had to take on the responsibility of shopping for groceries instead of my Amie. Therefore, I became more anxious because I feared catching the virus from outside and being cut off from my family.

On one occasion, while returning home with my car full of food items, I encountered a group of boys, some holding sticks, blocking my way just a few meters from my residence. They pleaded with me for help, telling me they were hungry and had no food. I asked to speak to their leader and requested that the rest of the group move away from my car. The boys agreed, and I talked to the leader alone, to whom I gave some money. They expressed their gratitude with profound cheers and prayers. However, the situation also made me worried about the possibility of public disorder due to the lack of food.

To cope with the constant news about COVID-19, I decided to limit my consumption of news channels and instead attend webinars that could teach me new skills applicable to my work. I teamed up with my friends, Musa Suwa and Salifu Bah, to begin hosting webinars for finance professionals in the Gambia. As our webinar gained popularity, along with other young Gambians, we transformed it into an elevated platform, the Finance Leadership Forum.

Furthermore, I took a course on data science using Python, which increased my understanding of data science and its related applications, like machine learning and artificial intelligence. As the work from home continued, I enrolled in a Management and Leadership Certificate Program with the Wharton School. These courses and activities prepared me for an uncertain future. The more I learned, the more I wanted diverse responsibilities so I could apply my new skills at work.

During that same year, the AFC investment division launched an internal learning platform called the AFC Academy. This academy aimed to facilitate training and knowledge-sharing events among the corporation's employees. The academy coordinator, Halima Ababa, invited me to help develop some of the course content and syllabus, and I happily agreed.

After several weeks of collaborative effort, I was asked to facilitate the first training session for the new academy. The course was titled "Business Applications of Microsoft Excel for Beginners." I was proud to be the first trainer to lead this inaugural training. It was so fulfilling to share my knowledge and skills with my colleagues. I felt valued as a contributor to the AFC Academy.

In retrospect, I see that my interest in learning and sharing knowledge grew as I personally developed. Hence, one of my favorite quotes is, "Personal development is a personal responsibility." Whatever I learn and share, I receive in return in some form or another.

CHAPTER TWENTY-ONE

RISE TO ARISE

As the novel virus spread, economies worldwide locked down, businesses had to close, and millions became concerned about their livelihoods. Like many others, I worried about the uncertain future, but not my job.

In the second quarter of 2020, a significant opportunity knocked on my door, one I had always dreamed of in my professional life. Before COVID-19 started, one of AFC's investee companies, ARISE, had been restructured into different verticals, including ARISE Ports & Logistics (APL) and ARISE Integrated Industrial Platforms (AIIP). APL consisted of three ports with a balance sheet of more than $1.1 billion and needed a CFO for the group. AFC was supposed to nominate someone for the role. Then, I was a Vice President for financial control and budgeting in AFC's finance division.

The opportunity was perfect for me to make a significant career pivot and take on a new challenge. Therefore, when my line Director advised me of the secondment opportunity, I received it with readiness. But before pursuing the discussion further, I needed to speak to my wife first. Amie and I discussed the benefits and challenges of the role and its location, which required us to move from Nigeria to Gabon. We eventually agreed to take on the opportunity.

Next, I spoke to my titan of mentors, who encouraged me to step out of my comfort zone and make a new impact, even if it meant working in a new sector. Nonetheless, they also warned me that it would require more work as I had no prior sector experience.

Despite my confidence in leading a team, as soon as I was asked to attend an interview, I felt apprehensive about my limited knowledge of the ports and logistics industry. It was an anxiety of responsibility with limited experience. The anxiety of moving out of my comfort zone. I began to protest the negative thoughts by telling myself, "*I have what it takes to be a CFO! My knowledge about the companies is an advantage.*" To prepare, I searched for reports and books on African ports and logistics industry. Halima Ababa, an excellent colleague in the investment division, also provided me with some materials to read.

Kim Fijer, the APL Board chairman, and Gagan Gupta, the founder of ARISE, interviewed me. We discussed strategy, leadership, business partnerships, and talent development. As a Toastmaster, I incorporated storytelling into my responses, sharing how I struggled to acquire an education and how I would use such an experience to support talent development and stakeholder management.

In June 2020, ARISE officially gave me the job as CFO of APL, and I was set to begin on August 20. I sought an audience with Ayotunde and Samaila, the CFO and CEO of AFC, respectively, to gain valuable input on becoming a strategic business partner in ARISE.

A week before my departure, my colleagues in AFC Finance threw a surprise send-forth dinner for me. While they were offering their comments and advice, I felt a rush of emotions. The reality hit me that I would be starting a new job where I would need to build new relationships with new people. I felt sad that I'd left behind great colleagues and memories of the evenings we spent eating "suya," roasted corn, and groundnut. But the fact that my new job was a secondment gave me some consolation.

I was scheduled to visit Gabon the following month. Getting a flight became another issue as nations were only beginning to open their doors again. I took a route I never imagined, flying British Airways from Lagos to London, then Air France to Paris, and finally Paris to Libreville. Traveling from Lagos to Libreville, two Central West African nations, took almost three days. The long experience reminded me of Africa's poor integration and made me wonder why African countries didn't open their borders to their neighbors but allowed flights from Europe. The solution to this question lies in the trust, relationships, and policies needed to improve regional integration in Africa. A solution that is core to the purpose of both ARISE & AFC's existence.

AT ARISE. On my first day at work, the receptionist greeted me with a warm smile, but her eyes were hidden behind a face mask, a constant reminder of the dangers we faced. She checked my temperature and handed me a bottle of hand sanitizer.

As I rode the elevator, I thought about how different this experience felt from my previous jobs. There were no handshakes or hugs from my new colleagues, no tour of the office, and no team lunch to break the ice. Instead, I was greeted by an empty desk, a laptop, and a packet of face masks.

But even as I settled into my new role, I couldn't shake off the feeling that *everything* was different. The world was changing, and so were our ways of working. I was grateful for the opportunity to start this new chapter in my life, but I wondered what the future holds for us all. Meanwhile, I had to make the best use of the hybrid working style available.

Like footballers who need to train even after winning tournaments, knowledge workers must also keep learning and improving their skills. This is especially important when starting a new role in a new industry. So, when I arrived in Gabon, I quickly developed two plans to help me learn about the ports and logistics industries.

First, I created a new CFO success plan for myself. This included all the documents and reports I should read, and people I needed to meet to understand the business. Second, I decided to take a distance-learning course on port key performance indicators (KPIs) from a school in London, which I self-sponsored. I felt that understanding how performance is measured in the industry would give me a good overview of which areas I needed to master quickly.

This strategy worked well for me. I learned how performance is measured in the ports, which enabled me to ask the right questions during business review meetings.

Fortunately, I had a supportive team to help me through my onboarding process, which would have been much more difficult without the assistance of Yash, a finance trainee, Andrew, the APL CEO, or Gagan Gupta, the Founder of ARISE. Additionally, I requested each of the three port finance managers to provide an induction that focused on how their company creates value and generates revenue.

As I settled into my new role, I became intrigued by its unfamiliar territory. Each day brought fresh opportunities to learn and grow, particularly in integration and stakeholder management. Working alongside colleagues from all corners of the world - Europe, Asia, America, and Africa - I was struck by the richness of our diversity, even at the board level.

Making tough decisions as we juggled competing priorities gave me a newfound appreciation for the complexity of leadership roles. Despite continuing to teach corporate governance to MBA students, I recognized that there was always more to learn. Hence, I joined the Institute of Directors London - to stay on top of the latest issues in the UK, where our company is registered, and to help me better navigate my role in the boardroom.

I also enrolled in a course with the Institute of Mergers and Acquisitions so I could play an active role during the transition period and ensure smooth and effective integration. Although these courses and memberships were self-sponsored, I knew they were worth the investment.

As the role of CFO constantly evolved, I recognized that strategic management remained a critical component of the job. In December of the following year, I decided to further my education in strategic matters by enrolling in a course on strategic CFO at Harvard Business School. This course proved incredibly valuable, as it covered contemporary issues and allowed me to network with other professionals in the field.

During the following quarter, I pursued a one-year diploma course on port management, which was recommended to me by Mr Gupta. This course further gave me a deeper understanding of port activities, governance, and other areas critical to the success of operations. With every new opportunity for learning and development, I took on more responsibilities in my role.

In 2022, I was promoted to Chief Operating Officer (COO) for ARISE P&L, in addition to my existing CFO function. Relocating to the ARISE Dubai Office, this new role expanded my involvement in critical stakeholder management, including the board and other shareholders of the subsidiaries.

When I looked back on my association with ARISE, I felt grateful for the decision and support that led me to join the company. It became a true barrier breaker for me, allowing me to move out of my comfort zone, work with diverse employees, and achieve significant growth in my professional career.

One of my proudest achievements came when I received the National Order of Knights from the Republic of Cote d'Ivoire. This award recognized the work my colleagues and I had done in developing a new seaport in San Pedro. Growing up in a small Saruja village with big dreams, I never imagined receiving such a prestigious award from a major nation like Côte d'Ivoire. It was a tremendous honor and privilege.

AFTERWORD

MY EXPERIENCE, YOUR LEARNING

This book is not the last chapter of my memories, but the start of a new life. As I pause to narrate my journey to acquire knowledge, I cannot help but look back at the beginning of my life. It's incredible to see how far I've come. Growing up in the village as a young boy, going to school felt like an impossible dream. But with purposeful hard work, determination, and the help of those around me, I finished school and achieved growth beyond what I had imagined.

There were some tough times along the way. There were days when I was kicked out of school or dropped out of university because I couldn't afford the fees. And there were nights when I went to bed hungry.

I often wonder what helped me move from a place of struggle to a place of betterment. It's hard to pinpoint just one thing, but a combination of factors played a role. First, the power of the prayers I had earned from my parents, family, and the people I met. Secondly, I always had hope. Even during tough times, I believed things would improve one day. I felt like God was showing me a bigger picture of my future, which gave me the strength to keep going. I also had a burning desire to change my circumstances, which kept me motivated and focused on my goals.

But I didn't do it alone. Some people believed in me and saw my potential, even when I couldn't. My parents worked hard to provide for our family and instilled strong life values in me. My teachers, colleagues, and mentors encouraged me to keep pushing, even when the odds were against me. And my friends and family stood by me through thick and thin. Thanks to their help, I went from running a small business with a donkey cart in the village to running a billion-dollar ports and logistics business and becoming the son of Africa.

My struggles were not in vain. I have learned many things, traveled to many countries, and grown in many ways. Those memories and experiences have shaped me into who I am today, and I will always carry them. They taught me the value of hard work, resilience, and relationships. They also sparked a passion for personal development, knowledge sharing, and social causes. I know that many people face similar challenges in life, and I want to help them in any way I can. That's why I co-founded two non-profit organizations that focused on education and other social causes, created blogs to share articles on financial literacy and business management, and taught thousands of youths in Africa in the classroom and online. I mentor anyone who wants to learn from my experiences and overcome their challenges. Through these efforts, I aim to positively impact other people's lives.

Education and personal development are the foundation of all these actions and changes. It has had the highest multiplier effect in my life. Therefore, I conclude that purposeful education is the best way to fight poverty or bring changes.

ACKNOWLEDGEMENTS

We are social beings, and our lives are shaped by other people. This story and the book would not have been possible without the presence of thousands of other people. Champions of education.

I extend my heartfelt gratitude to my family in Saruja, Brikamaba, Dasilameh, Jarumeh Koto, Tallinding, and Lamin. Lagos, Libreville & Dubai.

I am deeply thankful to the mentors, friends, and educators who crossed my path, shaping my journey through their wisdom and guidance. To all my colleagues in Ecobank, GTBank Gambia, Africa Finance Corporation, and ARISE Group.

A special thank you to those who helped document this tale – the editors, Scott Allan & the Self-Publishing School, and everyone involved. Your dedication has transformed my story into a narrative I hope will inspire others.

Finally, I would like to thank all the students and mentees I have known over the years. What an extraordinary privilege to be one of your partners. Thank you to the readers for taking the time to delve into my experiences. May my journey serve as a testament to the power of education, resilience, and community support.

READ MORE

Craving for more books from Ebrima Sawaneh

The book is a real eye-opener. I bought it some time ago, and a friend pinched it, so I bought myself a second copy. I want to mention that it can be used for all professions.
- Olimatou Chongan

If you'd like to be informed when my next books will be published, let me know. I will add your name to my friendship contact list. Visit ebrimasawaneh.com

FEEDBACK

Thank you for purchasing this book. I love feedback and would love to hear what you have to say. If you enjoyed this book, I'd like to ask you a big favor. What did you find useful about this book? Please post a review of this book on Amazon or Goodreads.

ABOUT THE AUTHOR

Ebrima Sawaneh is a bestselling author, CFO and social entrepreneur who is passionate about personal development and education. He serves as the COO & CFO of Arise Ports & Logistics. He has held senior finance roles at Africa Finance Corporation and Ecobank Gambia. Ebrima holds an MBA in Finance and has acquired executive education at Wharton School and Harvard Business School.

Ebrima is the President of the Next Generation Foundation and Finance Leadership Forum. In 2022, he received the Chevalier de L'Ordre Nationale from the Republic of Cote d'Ivoire in recognition of his contribution to the country. Ebrima resides in Dubai with his K-Family – (K)Amie, Kumba, Kebba, and Khadri.

ebrimasawaneh.com

www.ingramcontent.com/pod-product-compliance
Lightning Source LLC
LaVergne TN
LVHW091255080426
835510LV00007B/270